MACHINE LEARNING FOR BEGINNERS

A Comprehensive Guide To Algorithms

For Machine Learning And Data Science

WILLIAM J. FORD

Table of Contents

INTRODUCTION

Machine learning is an artificial intelligence (AI) subfield. The aim of machine learning is to understand the structure of data and to fit that data into models that people can understand and use.

Although machine learning is a domain of computer science, it varies from traditional computer methods. In traditional computing, algorithms include specifically programmed instructions for calculating or solving problems by computers. Alternatively, machine learning algorithms allow computers to train input data and use statistical analysis to produce values within a certain range. This makes it easier to create models of sample data by machines in order to simplify decision-making processes based on data inputs.

Today, any technology customer profits from machine learning. Facial recognition technology enables social media platforms to help users tag and share friends ' photos. The system for optical character recognition (OCR) transforms text images into moving form. Recommendation motors, powered by machine learning, recommend what films or TV shows are next based on the preferences of the user. Self-driving cars based on computer control will soon be available to customers.

You know, after the first attempt that you have poured too much effort into it. You know that after the second attempt, you are near to the goal, but you must that the throwing angle. What happens here is that we learn something after every step and improve the end result. We are expected to benefit from our practice.

This implies that the activities involved with machine learning are basically computational rather than cognitively describing the area. In his article "Computer Machinery and Intelligence," which answered the question, "Do robots think?"Is the problem substituted" Could robots do what we (as thought entities) can do?""Machine learning is used in data analysis to devise the complex models and algorithms that are predictive; this is known as predictive analytics in commercial use. Such analytical models enable academics, data scientists, technicians, and analysts to "produce accurate, consistent judgments and outcomes" and to uncover "secret insights" through learning from past relationships and input patterns.

Suppose you want to try out this holiday bid. You visit the website of the travel agency to search for a room. If you glance at a particular hotel, there is a segment underneath the overview of the hotel named "You may like these hotels, too." This is a widely encountered example of "Recommendation Machine" machine learning. Once again, several data points have been used to train a model to determine which hotels should view you in this segment based on lots of knowledge you already care about.

When, for example, you want the software to forecast traffic patterns in a busy crossing (Task T), you can put them through an algorithm for machine learning with data from past traffic patterns (experience E) and, if it's effectively "learned," it's going to do well to predict future traffic patterns (performance P).

The highly complex complexity of many real-world issues also ensures that it is unworkable, if not impractical, to develop sophisticated formulas that will solve them seamlessly at all times. Types of issues of machine learning include, "Is this cancer?"Which one of these people are good friends?"Is this person going to like this film?"Such problems are excellent targets for machine learning, and machine learning has actually been successfully implemented with such problems.

Machine learning is an ever-changing environment. It offers you several aspects to take into account when interacting with machine learning methodologies or when evaluating the effects of machine learning systems.

Machine Learning is, without a doubt, one of the most powerful and influential technologies in the world today. Above all, we are far from seeing its full potential. It will continue to make news for the foreseeable future; there is no doubt. This article is meant as an introduction to the basics of machine learning that addresses all basic ideas without being too large.

Machine learning is an instrument for translating information into intelligence. There has been an influx of data in the last 50 years. This amount of data is worthless if we do not examine it and identify the trends inside. Machine learning approaches are used to recognize the useful underlying trends automatically inside complicated data, which we would otherwise find difficult. The hidden patterns and knowledge of a problem can be used to predict future events and make complex decisions of all types.

We are drowning and hungry for knowledge— John Naisbitt Most of us do not know that we interact each day with machine learning. Through when we listen to an album or take a picture, Google Machine Learning is part of the engine behind it, constantly learning from each experience and improving. It is also behind advances that change the world, such as cancer detection, new medicines and self-driving automobiles.

HISTORY OF MACHINE LEARNING

From the start, scientists who follow Blaise Pascal and Von Leibniz have been reflecting on a machine that is as much intellectually as human. Well-known artists such as Jules Verne, Frank Baum (Wizard of OZ), Marry Shelly (Frankenstein), George Lucas (Star Wars) were thinking about intelligent creatures with human behaviors.

Machine learning is one of the important pathways of AI, an extremely spicy hot topic in research or industry. Universities and corporations commit numerous resources for developing their awareness. Recent developments in the area contribute to very strong results for various tasks, equivalent to human performance (98.98 percent for traffic signs-higher than human-).

Here I would like to share a crude Machine Learning schedule and to sign some of the milestones. You should also apply "to my understanding" to the start of any statement in the letter.

Hebb proposed the first step towards prevalent ML in 1949 on the basis of a neuropsychological study formulation. It is named Hebbian philosophy of thinking. This describes associations between the nodes of the Recurrent Neural Network (RNN) with a simple explanation. It stores all commonalities on the network and later serves as a memory. The argument states that: Let us presume that a cell A axon is close enough for a cell B to excite and that it is shot again and again or again by an onset of growth process or metabolic shift in one or both of the cells so that it is effective; let's assume that the presence or the occurrence of a reversing operation (or trace) tends to lead to permanent cellular changes that add to its stability...

Arthur Samuel developed a program for Checkers at IBM in 1952. The software has been able to observe positions and develop a pattern that provides better movements in the latter situations. Samuel played so many games with the system and found it could perform better over time.

With this project, Samuel confused the devices which govern the general providence with the written codes and learn models such as the human being. He invented "machine learning," which he described as a study area, which gives computers the skill without being programmed directly.

F. Rosenblatt

In 1957, the second model introduced by Rosenblatt's Perceptron, again with neuroscientific history, is more similar to today's ML models. At that moment, it was a very interesting development and practically extended more than Hebbian's theory. Designed by Rosenblatt with the following lines, the perceptron describes some of the fundamental characteristics of intelligent systems in general, without becoming too closely involved with special conditions that are often obscure and include individual biological species.

After 3 years, Widrow developed the Delta Training law, which is then used for Perceptron preparation as realistic practice. It is also known as the problem of Least Square. Combining these two ideas creates a good linear classification. But the enthusiasm of Perceptron was hanged by Minsky in 1969. He suggested the well-known XOR problem and Perceptrons ' inability to handle such linearly inseparable data distributions. It was the Minsky's solution to NN. Thereafter, NN work would be dormant up until the 80s XOR problem, not linearly separable knowledge, until the Werbos ' 1981 intuition of Multi-Layer perceptron (MLP) with the NN basic backpropagation(BP) algorithm was suggested, although the BP concept had previously been proposed by Linnainmaa in 1970, under the heading "reverse automatic differentiation mode." Even BP is the key component in NN architecture today. NN work has expanded again with these new ideas. In 1985-1986, NN researchers subsequently put forward the idea of MLP with practical BP training (Rumelhart, Hinton, Williams-Hetch, Nielsen). On the other hand, J. R. Quinlan proposed a very well-known ML algorithm in 1986, which we call Decision Trees, specifically ID 3 algorithm.

One of the most important advances in ML was Vector Support Machines (SVM), which Vapnik and Cortes proposed[10] in 1995 with very high theoretical and empirical performance. That was the time to

7

separate the ML community into two crowds as advocates of NN or SVM. The rivalry between the two groups, however, was not very simple for the NN side following the Kernelized SVM version in about 2000s (I was unable to locate the first paper about the topic), SVM had the best of many NN models ' tasks before. SVM was also able to leverage all the information of convex optimization, generalization principle of margin, and kernels toward NN models. It could, therefore, find a wide push from various disciplines, which could lead to rapid theoretical and practical improvements.

NN sought more claims from Hochreiter's work in 1991, and Hochreiter et al. .in 2001; the depletion of NN units indicates gradient failure as we use BP information. It simply means that after a certain number of times, it is unnecessary to train NN units due to saturated systems, and therefore NNs are very likely to overfit in a few epochs.

In 1997 Freund and Schapire suggested another solid type of ML recommended with a large ensemble of poor classifiers called Adaboost. The contributors were also given the Godel Award. Adaboost trains a limited collection of simple to train classifiers that give greater priority to difficult circumstances. This pattern also forms the basis of various activities such as face recognition and identification. It also follows the PAC (probably roughly correct) principle of learning. In general, so-called poor classifiers (single decision tree nodes) are used for simple decisions. They implemented Adaboost as the model we research can be viewed as the broad, abstract addition to the general decision-theoretical framework of the well known on-line prediction model...

Another ensemble model, explored by Breiman in 2001, combines various decision-making bodies, in which each of them is selected from a random sub-package of instances. It is called Random Forests(RF) because of its nature. RF also has theoretical and empirical evidence of tolerance to overfitting. Also, AdaBoost reveals that the over-fit and outer instances of data are low; RF is a more reliable model against these safeguards. RF also demonstrates its success in many different tasks, such as Kaggle competitions.

Random forests are a mixture of tree predictors that each tree relies on the values of an individually and equally distributed random vector sampled on all forest trees. The common forest mistake converges a.s. To a limited extent, as the number of trees in the forest increases, a new era of NN called Deep Learning has been commercialized as we are entering today. This statement simply refers to NN structures with many layers in sequence. The third NN increase started around 2005 with a synthesis of several observations by recent mavens including Hinton, LeCun, Bengio, Andrew Ng, and other important older scholars from past and present. Some of the essential headings I have enlisted;

- ✓ GPU programming
- ✓ Convolutional NNs
- ✓ Deconvolutional Networks

- ✓ Optimization algorithms
- ✓ Stochastic Gradient Descent
- ✓ BFGS and L-BFGS
- ✓ Conjugate Gradient Descent
- ✓ Backpropagation
- ✓ Rectifier Units
- ✓ Sparsity
- ✓ Dropout Nets
- ✓ Maxout Nets
- ✓ Unsupervised NN models
- ✓ Deep Belief Networks
- ✓ Stacked Auto-Encoders
- ✓ Denoising NN models

Combining all of these concepts with those not identified, NN models will address state-of-the-art challenges such as object recognition, speech recognition, or NLP. It should be remembered, though, that this does not imply anything, it is the end of other ML sources. While positive Deep Learning stories are growing fast, many critiques are pointed at cost training and the tuning of these models ' exogenous parameters. Nevertheless, owing to its usability, SVM is still more widely used.

I have to focus on a relatively young ML pattern before I do. BigData has arisen and influenced ML work dramatically amid the rise of WWW and social media. Thanks to BigData's large problems, many good ML algorithms are ineffective for rational systems (of course, not for big tech companies). Thus, the researchers develop a new set of simple models known as bandit algorithms that render learning simpler and more adaptable for large-scale problems.

So, where are we headed next in machine learning history?

We are building individuality and artificial intelligence in general.

Until date, AI and machine learning have been confined to the resolution of specific issues.

The more general development of A.I. The next limit is the ability to perform multiple tasks and to solve various types of problems with one system.

In fact, Sentient A.I is seen as the next boundary. The device could, therefore, be built and upgraded without human interference.

THE MOST COMMON MACHINE LEARNING TERMS, EXPLAINED

"Machine learning" is one of the present technology buzzwords, frequently used in parallel with an expert system, deep learning, and big information; however, what does it really suggest? And what other machine learning terminology is important to comprehend?

McKinsey has defined machine learning as "algorithms that can gain from data without depending on rules-based programming." Carnegie Mellon University provides this: "The field of Machine Learning seeks to respond to the concern 'How can we build computer system systems that automatically enhance with experience, and what are the basic laws that govern all discovering procedures?'".

Machine learning indicates that the precision of the system is enhancing gradually, with the addition of more data and feedback. You probably experience lots of examples of machine learning every day without recognizing it. When Facebook suggests "individuals you may know," or when Amazon emails you suggestions of items you may like based upon previous purchases, they are utilizing machine learning algorithms to tailor your results.

Machine learning deepens the work of an expert system. In AI, researchers initially developed rules for computer systems to make decisions. With machine learning, computer systems really "learn" for themselves and design new rules through practice and repeating.

Finding Out Algorithms.

From medical diagnoses to scams detection, machine learning is improving our ability to resolve social issues. Paypal got the ML start-up Simility to analyze millions of transactions and flag anomalies to prevent cash laundering. Machine learning can likewise predict hypoxemia (low oxygen levels) during surgery; acknowledge cardiovascular danger aspects like hypertension, age, and smoking cigarettes in retinal images; and identify abnormal growths during colonoscopies.

Embracing machine learning at scale is not without obstacles. Machine learning can result in overfitting (when the machine anticipates outcomes based on historical data but does not adjust to new variables), and sometimes it is tough to find large enough information samples for the machines to train with.

Although lots of people fret about ML replacing individuals, devices, and humans complement each other in many ways. According to the Harvard Business Review, "through ... collaborative intelligence, humans and AI actively enhance each other's complementary strengths: the leadership, team effort, imagination, and social abilities of the former, and the speed, scalability, and quantitative capabilities of the latter.".

Human beings can assist train and run devices and explain their habits. When Microsoft established the ML bot Cortana, it needed substantial data points and human insights to create a personality that was "confident, caring, and helpful, however not bossy." A poet, a novelist, and a playwright were all part of the team that trained the bot on how to interact successfully with people.

Machine learning has plenty of intriguing variants and subfields, so let's start translating other machine learning terms.

Machine Learning Terminology.

Classification is a part of monitored knowing (knowing with identified data) through which information inputs can be easily separated into classifications. In machine learning, there can be binary classifiers with only 2 outcomes (e.g., spam, non-spam) or multi-class classifiers (e.g., types of books, animal species, and so on).

Among the most popular classification algorithms is a choice tree, where repeated questions causing exact categories can build an "if-then" framework for limiting the pool of possibilities in time.

Clustering.

Clustering is a kind of unsupervised knowing (knowing with unlabeled information) that includes organizing data points according to features and qualities.

Clustering can be utilized to arrange customer demographics and acquiring habits into particular segments for targeting and product positioning. It can likewise analyze real estate quality and geographic locations to produce realty valuations and plan the layout of brand-new city developments. It can categorize details by topics within libraries or web pages and put together a quickly available directory for users.

The most typical kind of clustering is K-means clustering, which involves representing each cluster by a variable "k" and then specifying the centroid of those clusters. All data points are then assigned to a specific cluster, and, through this procedure, we identify the centroid of the brand-new clusters. Here are a few examples of what K-means clustering looks like in practice:

A hospital wants to locate emergency units at the minimum possible range from areas where accidents often occur.

A seismologist studies regions where earthquakes have actually taken place over the last few years to recognize the locations of greatest danger.

A pizzeria wants to comprehend where to find stores based upon customer demand to reduce the range the chauffeurs need to travel for shipment.

Other clustering approaches that you can find out more about here consist of density-based clustering, hierarchical-based methods, segmenting methods, and grid-based approaches.

Regressions.

Regressions produce relationships and correlations between different types of information. For example, each profile picture has an image with pixels that belong to a person. With static prediction (one that remains the very same over time), machine learning acknowledges that a certain pixel arrangement corresponds to a provided name and allows for a facial acknowledgment (for instance, when Facebook suggests tags for the images you've just published).

Regressions can also work when forecasting outcomes based upon information in today. For a very long time, statistical regression has been used to resolve problems, such as predicting the healing of cognitive functions after a stroke or forecasting customer churn in the telecom industry. The only difference is that now a number of these regression analyses can be done more effectively and rapidly by machines.

Regression is a kind of structured machine learning algorithm where we can label the inputs and outputs. Linear regression provides outputs with constant variables (any value within a range), such as rates information. Logistical regression is when variables are unconditionally reliant, and the labeled variables are specifically defined. For example, you can categorize whether a store is open as (1) or (0), but there are just two possibilities.

Other kinds of regression that you can explore here are polynomial regression, support vector regression, decision tree regression, and random forest regression.

Deep Learning.

Deep learning is similar to machine learning-- in fact, it's more of an application of machine learning that imitates the workings of the human brain. Deep learning networks interpret huge data (information that is too large to fit on a single computer)-- both unstructured and structured-- and recognize patterns. The more data they can "find out" from, the more educated and precise their decisions will be. Here are some examples of deep learning in practice:

Chatbots and virtual assistants: Virtual assistants like Alexa and Siri or customer care chatbots on various web pages can get human demands, analyze language, and present lifelike reactions.

Real-time bidding and programmatic marketing: Advertising now depends upon the software application buying advertising area through a competitive bidding process. Cognitive AI is an example of a deep learning platform that synthesizes information on consumer demographics, weather conditions, offered stock, time of day, and other variables to produce custom purchasing algorithms for a particular target market.

Recommendation engines: From travel sites like Booking.com and Expedia to streaming platforms like Netflix and Spotify, suggestion engines learn from previous acquiring or user behavior to personalize marketing. There are 2 kinds of recommendation engines: collective, where user choice data is collected at scale and users are compared to similar user personas, and content-based filtering, where properties of particular products are evaluated and future products are compared to past items to figure out the closest matches.

Neural Networks

Neural networks are closely linked with profound understanding. They construct serial neuronal layers to facilitate understanding of data from a machine in order to provide accurate analysis.

A neural network consists of node layers which are activated by "cause" data. Such knowledge is then weighted by coefficients, as certain data inputs may be more essential than others.

The neurons usually occur in three different layers: an input data sheet, a secret data measurement layer, and an output layer. In a case in point where we want to quantify the price of airline tickets, our entry layer will gather airports of origin, destination, exit, and airlines. -obtained a weight (maybe the departure date is more relevant than the airline) and then a price forecast will follow.

Natural Language Processing

The AI subfield that handles human languages is natural language processing. The problem is that human language is often not absolute. There are expressions, phrases, or sentences that are unique to certain dialects and communities, and sentences with grammar and punctuation may take on different definitions. Similar to human communications, the processors of natural languages have to make correct definitions using the syntax (arranging words) and semantics (the meaning of that arrangement).

The first step in natural language processing is to convert unstructured language data into a computer-readable form. The computer then translates each sentence in algorithms, often in a different form (for example, speech to text or language to language).

Language processing can support localization apps such as Google Translate, Slack, and Microsoft Word text sharing and interactive devices and virtual assistants. Here is an overview of how the Royal Bank of Scotland uses text analytics to evaluate correspondence, survey, and call center feedback from customer service to identify problem areas and to strengthen their engagement and credibility.

Machine Vision

Computer vision is the method by which computers can acquire and interpret pictures. This makes it possible to diagnose skin cancer by looking at X-rays and other medical images and to detect traffic and vehicle types in auto cars in real-time such as the new models from Tesla.

Machines can "see" in many different ways: numerically represent colors, divide images into various parts, and identify corners, edges, and textures. When the machines gather and code more details, they start to see the bigger picture.

Many of the trends in machine vision today encompass integration into the industry's internet, the collection of productivity inputs and sensory data at factories and non-industrial applications such as "drivers ' cars, autonomous agricultural equipment, drone applications, smart traffic systems, and guided operations."

Key Elements of Machine Learning

Tens of thousands of machine learning algorithms are available, and hundreds of new algorithms are developed annually.

Every machine learning algorithm has three components: representation. Examples include decision trees, rulesets, cases, visual structures, neural networks, vector machines support, software assemblies, and others.

Evaluation: how applicant systems are tested (hypotheses). Examples include precision, forecast, and warning, squared error, likelihood, subsequent chance, rate, margin, the divergence between entropy and kL, etc.

Optimization: the creation of applicant services, defined as the search process. Combinatorial optimization, convex optimization, restricted optimization, for example.

Such three elements are incorporated in all machine learning algorithms. A structure for all algorithms to learn.

Machine Learning Engineer

Who is responsible for applying ML inside organizations with all these thrilling technological developments? In many instances, the primary responsibility rests with the programmer, a data-driven software engineer who constructs applications to understand and do work independently. In addition, such developers will know different codebases, distributed processing, technology conflict and computer science.

Here is a Springboard snapshot of what is required to become a leading engineer. And here's a machine learning engineer's description.

Machine learning is growing, with 96% of firms raising their expenditure in this sector by 2020. In reality, machine learning has been projected to increase the number 1 in-demand AI capabilities, and the global market is expected to seven times more from $1.4 billion in 2017 to $8.8 billion in 2022.

The low talent pool–according to Element AI, there are less than 10,000 people worldwide with the necessary skills–is one of the main challenges for machine learning today. This ensures that people with the right qualifications will profit from fair wages and job stability.

TYPES OF MACHINE LEARNING ALGORITHMS

M achine learning has become a robust and diversified business tool that strengthens many aspects of the business.

The effect on business performance can be so important that machine learning systems must be applied in many fields and sectors to maintain productivity.

Machine learning is a crucial step in business activities involving a great deal of energy. It is, therefore important to realize what your company wants ML to do and how different types of ML algorithms operate.

In this section, we will discuss the main types of machine learning algorithms, explain their function, and understand the benefits.

Supervised Algorithms Machine Learning

Supervised Algorithms provide direct oversight of the process. In this case, the author codes sample data and set strict constraints on which the algorithm performs.

To understand supervised learning algorithms, first look at the example: Suppose there are two ships, ships A and B, and both carry a large number of cars. On ship A, the vehicles are all numbered in a folder, but they are not on shipB. Then think finding each car on the ship B and marking it in the database is somebody's task. The approach is to build a model based on data from Ship A and then adapt it to data from Ship B. For example, he learns from ship A that cars with four wheels and over four seats are SUVs. He may state that he is using this information to identify cars such as SUVs on ship B.

Controlled learning is this paradigm in a nutshell. It is a sort of machine learning that seeks a solution based on data you already have for the present problem.

More technically speaking, guided learning is a form of machine learning algorithm that evolves a model or method based on input-output pairs in the training data, so as to map the input from the test data to their respective output. Training details, also called the training dataset, are a database of market data, and the test data or the test data set is an unmarked input set. One aspect we can see is that supervised learning can be described as a kind of machine learning that allows an instructor to have training data technically speaking.

Controlled learning is further classified into two subtypes: regression and controlled classification. Regression applies to a supervised learning process, where all data are numerical (or permanent) values.

Classification methods, by comparison, utilize categorical meanings that are usually linear (0 or 1).

Two major problems in supervised learnings are:

Commitment to bias-variance: Such equations from with assumptions and variance parameters, which can lead to problems. Biases can cause errors in the results, as they are based rather than the data itself on assumptions concerning the data. Variance, particularly high variance, can lead to models performing well on data, but poorly on data testing.

Data noise: data errors can contribute to the uncertainty of the system.

It's a spoonful variant of machine learning, whatever kind of knowledge performance you pick (samples) to "use" the algorithm, which kind of outcomes you like (for example, "yes / no" or "true / false").

From the point of view of the computer, this method is more or less a ritual to connect the dots.

Supervised learning primarily aims to scale data range and predict data that are unavailable, future, or unavailable on the basis of labeled sample data.

Supervised machine learning includes two major processes:

Classification And Regression.

Classification is the process where incoming data are labeled using previous data samples and manually trains the algorithm to recognize

24

and categorize certain types of objects accordingly. The machine must be able to differentiate information forms to carry out a visual character, picture, or conditional acknowledgment (whether a certain bit of data is "yes" or "no" in compliance with certain requirements).

Regression is the mechanism by which trends are defined, and cumulative results are measured. The system must know the numbers, its values, groupings (e.g., heights and widths), etc.

The most widely used supervised algorithms are:

- ✓ Linear Regression;
- ✓ Logistical Regression;
- ✓ Random Forest;
- ✓ Gradient Boosted Trees;
- ✓ Support Vector Machines (SVM);
- ✓ Neural Networks;
- ✓ Decision Trees;
- ✓ Naive Bayes;
- ✓ Nearest Neighbor.

Supervised Learning Algorithms Use Cases

Price forecast and pattern forecasting in revenue, retail trade, and stock trading are the main areas of use for supervised research. An algorithm utilizes incoming data in both situations to determine the probability and measure potential results.

The best examples are sales enabling platforms such as Seismic and Highspot that use an algorithm of this kind to present various possible scenarios.

Overviewed learning business cases involve ad tech activities as part of an ad advertising chain. The task of a supervised learning algorithm is to determine potential ad space prices and their importance during the bidding process in real-time, while also restricting budget spending (for example, the price range of a single purchase and the overall budget for a specific time).

Unsupervised Machine Learning Algorithms

Consider the following example to help understand uncontrolled learning algorithms:

Instead of two ships, ships A and B, there is only one ship carrying several types of fruits, although you do not know the types of fruits it carries. The alternative is to break the products of the ship into classes on the basis of their physical characteristics. You can, for example, divide by color, then by size, then form, etc. Essentially, this is how unattended learning models work.

To put it more formally, unregulated learning is a form of machine learning, which uses inferences taken from a dataset without labeling. The most common type of unregulated learning is clustering, which can be described as a mechanism by which hide patterns or clusters in data occur during the scanning process. In other terms, unattended learning algorithms can be viewed as a paradigm that can learn from test data rather than from an instructor or training data.

Uncontrolled learning does not involve the developer's direct control. Unless you know the results and have to arrange the details, then the desired results are unpredictable and still to be determined in the case of unregulated machine learning algorithms.

Another major difference between these two is that controlled learning primarily uses labeled data, whereas unregulated learning uses unlabeled data.

The unregulated machine learning algorithm is used to:

- ✓ Explore the knowledge structure;
- ✓ Gain valuable insights;
- ✓ Identify patterns;
- ✓ Apply this to increase efficiency.

In other words, unattended machine learning describes information by scan and understanding.

Unsupervised learning algorithms apply the following techniques to describe the data:

Clustering: an investigation of relevant classes of data used for segmentation (i.e., clusters) based on their internal structures, without previous knowledge of community authorization. The credentials are described by the similarities between data artifacts and their discrepancies (which can also be used to distinguish defects).

Reduction in dimensionality: there is a lot of noise in the incoming data. Machine learning algorithms use reduced-dimensionality to eliminate this noise during the distillation of relevant information.

The most popular algorithms used are:

- ✓ k-means clustering;
- ✓ t-SNE (t-Distributed Stochastic Neighbor Embedding);
- ✓ PCA (Principal Component Analysis);
- ✓ Association rule.

Use Cases of Unsupervised Learning Algorithms

Digital marketing and ad-technology are the fields of uncontrolled learning. In fact, this method is often used to analyze and modify customer information.

The problem is that in the incoming data, there are a number of so-called "known unknowns." The very efficiency of the company business depends on the ability to understand undeclared data and to extract relevant insights from it.

Modern data processing is packed with unattended algorithms. Lotame and Salesforce are currently amongst the most advanced platforms for data management that implement this ML algorithm.

Unattended learning can, therefore, be used to classify target audience groupings on the basis of certain attributes (be it behavioral details, personal data features, specific software context or other). This algorithm can be used to develop more effective ad content targeting and to identify campaign performance patterns.

Semi-supervised Machine Learning Algorithms

Semi-controlled learning algorithms are a middle ground between supervised and unregulated algorithms. In fact, the semi-controlled approach puts together some elements of both.

This is how semi-controlled algorithms work: Semi-controlled machine learning algorithms use a limited set of sample data to form the operational requirements (i.e., train itself).

The constraint contributes to a partially trained model, which later has the job of labeling the unlabeled results. The findings are known to be pseudo-labeled data because of the constraints of the research dataset.

Ultimately, marked and pseudo-marked sets of data are merged, producing a distinct algorithm that incorporates concise and statistical features of controlled and unmonitored learning.

Semi-supervised learning uses the classification process to identify and group data assets into separate sections.

Semi-supervised Machine Learning Use Cases

Among other items, the legal and health sectors handle web content recognition, image analysis, and voice processing with the aid of semi-managed software.

Semi-controlled learning is extended to crawling engines and content aggregation schemes in the case of the web content classification. In both instances, a wide range of symbols is used to classify and organize material in certain settings. However, for further classification, this procedure usually requires human input.

An excellent example is classify. GATE (General Architecture for Text Engineering) is another well-known tool for this category.

In the case of image and speech analysis, a marking of an algorithm is done to provide a valid image or speech processing model with a coherent, sample-based transcription. It can, for instance, be an MRI or a CT scan. With a small set of exemplary scans, a coherent model can be provided which identifies anomalies in the images.

Reinforcement Machine Learning Algorithms

Strengthening computing accounts for what is widely known as machine learning.

In general, enhanced learning is about creating an autonomous system, focused on the synthesis of labeled data and encounters with incoming data that is developed over coherent sequences of trials and failures.

Reinforced ML utilizes the exploration / exploitation approach. The principles are simple: the action takes place, the outcomes are measured, and the next action takes into account the effects of the first operation.

Reinforcement learning algorithms are reward signals that occur when certain tasks are performed. Reward cues are, in some cases, used to control the reward algorithms. You owe it an idea of the right and wrong course.

Reinforcement models are very similar to the way a dog is trained by someone. In other phrases, the reason you train a dog is when it completes a mission. The dog is represented by an agent in these algorithms, and the doggie treatment represents the prize. First, there's the task or the mission you want your dog to do. First, the setting and the translator are two important elements. One should recognize that the dog completes the aim duties and the human who controls and supports the dog with therapies, respectively.

Two main types of reward signals are:

Positive signal encourages constant execution of a specific action

Negative signal penalizes for certain actions and advises the algorithm to avoid penalties.

Nevertheless, according to the nature of the information, the role of the incentive signal may differ. Therefore compensation signals may be further categorized according to operational requirements. Generally, the program aims to optimize positive benefits and mitigate the negative effects.

The most popular learning algorithms for reinforcement include:

- ✓ Q-Learning;
- ✓ Temporal Difference (TD);
- ✓ Monte-Carlo Tree Search (MCTS);
- ✓ Asynchronous Actor-Critic Agents (A3C).

Use Cases for Reinforced Machine Learning Algorithms

Reinforcement Machine Learning suits minimal or contradictory knowledge. An algorithm can then construct its operating procedures on the basis of data encounters and related processes.

This type of machine learning model is widely used in modern NPCs and other video games. Reinforcement Learning helps the AI to adapt to player behavior and therefore provides realistic tasks. For example, this type of ML algorithm is used for moving vehicles and people in the Grand Theft Auto series.

Cars that drive themselves often rely on improved learning algorithms. If the self-driving car (e.g., Waymo) detects the road turn to the left, the "left turn" scenario may be activated, etc.

The most famous example of this deviation is AlphaGo, who went head to head with the world's second-best Go Player to over-play it by measuring the action sequences out of the current board location.

Marketing and marketing tech processes, on the other hand, also use reinforcement learning. This kind of algorithm of machine learning will allow re-targeting much more robust and effective by closely applying it to the actions and the context of the app

In addition, enhancement is used to amplify and adjust natural language processing (NLP) and chatbots dialog to:

Imitate the theme of the message

Create more appealing, insightful forms of responses

Find relevant answers according to the user feedback.

When Google DialogFlow was developed, such a bot became more of an Ui task than a technological achievement.

Machine learning can be categorized into three main types, including controlled learning, unattended learning, and improving learning. The labels of test data can be predicted for supervised models by training a model based on training data labels. Supervised learning methods can be categorized into models of regression and classification based on the type of data used. Unattended models of learning require that we find in the data hidden patterns and groups without the aid of training data. Finally, reinforcement learning models can be described as an agent who carries out tasks based on rewards in an environment.

WHAT MACHINE LEARNING CAN DO FOR YOUR BUSINESS AND HOW TO FIGURE IT OUT

M L investment was like mobile investing ten years Ago— it can transform your market

The quest for existing data is a well-known and widely accepted area. But ML is the next limit in data analysis. It is a science in which computer programs forecast or draw conclusions based on patterns they find through data and can develop insights through knowledge— without people telling them directly how. Since organizations have access to more data, machine learning allows them to obtain insights into the data at a scale, from single-user interaction to global trends and their impact on the planet. The use of these insights can also range from the individual pixel level experience to the creation of new products and business opportunities that currently do not exist. Remember that with ML, you can go much further with internal data— it is often possible to increase the power of ML by combining external data internally to generate new ideas that were not previously possible.

Frank Chen from A16Z has an excellent introduction to the potential applications of artificial intelligence, many of which require or need machine education. Some of these projects look to the future and are not yet practical for existing technologies, but provide a strong sense of possibility.

Just as consumers began thinking of investing in mobile 8–10 years ago, now is the time for companies to start exploring ML as a technology capable of helping to drive business results. To businesses that use current ML technology, there are various key topics for what ML can do. These are not comprehensive or identical, but instead represent different ways of thinking about your business ' potential impact: mass consumer configuration, feedback, and the device reaction. Imagine that everything a person does or sees can be tailored to their specific needs and behaviors. This includes recommendations for products or services classified as relevant to them, tailored user experience or flows based on user knowledge, their behavior, other people like them, or external data, including forecasts of what they would like to do next, etc. etc. This could mean the content is tailored to groups of consumers rather than people on a smaller scale.

The capacity to recognize items visually and simplify or customize interactions appropriately. Currently, technologies can recognize items, like live cams, in photographs and videos. Pinterest uses this to recommend similar / complementary items to those on an image the consumer is watching; Facebook uses face recognition technology to indicate friends be added into a photo; Amazon uses visual identity technology to build an automated shop check-out.

Automatic content recovery, generation, or processing. ML enables massive content in the world to be processed expeditiously. Common uses include document retrieval — for example finding all documents relevant to legal cases (note that it goes beyond keywords to searching for context), the classification of documents by topics and keywords, automated content summaries, extracting the relevant information from large quantities of content — for example finding specific terms in sales contracts, etc.

Scale forecasts, estimates, and trends. ML allows for forecasts that are very costly or hard to make otherwise. ML is particularly useful in making predictions which otherwise require a high level of expertise such as the cost of a house, or which are even impossible for a person to make such content in social media. Machines can also identify data trends well before they are evident to humans.

Unusual behavior or device error identification. Every system has problems and problems, but ML allows you not only to detect if problems arise but also whether these problems are unusual and alarming. This is especially useful in different surveillance and security systems.

From a strategic standpoint, ML can lead to a number of business outcomes: increased customer experience and functionality. Product customization is most popular— identifying the items that are most likely to be relevant for your consumers most quickly and efficiently, for example, their favorite matches on dating sites, albums, which they may want to purchase on music sites or goods, etc. The other case uses predictions to get the knowledge of entities or situations that they would not otherwise have. This may be general — for example. Zillow's Zestimate values a house the same irrespective of who looks at it, or adapts it to the customer— e.g., the rate a user gives will probably not give a film given their particular tastes.

External structures, business processes, and reasoning. Computer education can save you time and increase the efficiency of your resource investment in business processes and decisions. For starters, a loan company wants to maximize its engagement with prospective lending applications. It must decide who would like a loan to accept it if given but will still be willing to repay it. Prioritizing the most creditable consumers is not necessarily the answer, since customers usually have many choices and are less willing than others to sell, therefore creating a more complex model.

Additional vertical development and new products. Data can help you open up new business opportunities completely–create brand new products for your existing clients or serve segments or clients you haven't served before. For instance, by selling information from Netflix about which concepts and storylines perform for the market, Netflix may support theaters that are not the main target audience. Zillow can also allow real estate developers to realize which buildings can give them the best return on investments.

The determination of which region should first be concerned with relies on the possible business effect as well as the complexity and cost of the issue.

"We Need to Do Something with Our Data" Is a Strategy, Not a Data Science, Problem

Many companies want to recruit data scientists and people who create ML models, as "we should do something with our data." I have had several executives of influential companies say, "we see that our rivals purchase results, so we need to do that to remain competitive" and then recruit a number of data scientists who hope to create some magic. This leads me to a big misunderstanding of ML.

ML isn't the company's magic wand. The first task in ML is to recognize the effect of the technologies on companies. ML is a remedy— you first have to define the problem: What are your company findings for ML? How can ML help the customers? ML is a hammer— but a hammer isn't particularly useful if you don't have a nail. ML is an extremely varied collection of hammers to extend the cliche even further, and the kind of nail you have decides what hammer you're going to choose and how you will use it. The exact dilemma you are trying to solve is what determines the result, what your model will forecast, what the data you gather and analyze, and what algorithms you check and many other things should be optimized.

"Which question are we addressing at its core?"It is a business question, which means that product managers and business leaders ultimately have to define it, not the data scientists. Data scientists and other stakeholders will actively contribute to the concept— just do not challenge them and expect answers. If you have details with which you don't know what to do, perform client assessments, and talk about other clients throughout the company. Data scientists will help you analyze the data, generate your theories and iterate, but it would be impossible for them to build the case on their own unless they have a lot of problem space experience. To maximize the ML's value for the company, you need continuous cooperation between product managers and data scientists where product managers are responsible for ensuring that the problems resolved are the most impactful for the company.

How ML Can Move Your Business Forward Unpacking

While the possibilities of ML are infinite, you may wonder how the application will relate to your organization. Some examples are as follows:

Internal Processes

Where in my business are people today contributing expertise to automatic decision-making, so their abilities can be best used elsewhere?

What are the data people in my company usually scan, capture, or manually retrieve from certain knowledge sources and how can this be automated?

What are the decisions that people make in my company? Can those decisions be made by a machine if all the data my people have magically ingested?

-aspects of my customer interactions are developed by humans and can be theoretically adapted to machines??

Do I have a consistent consumer segmentation focused on their interests, actions, and needs? Is my product / expertise tailored to each segment?

Can I personalize the experience for each individual customer based on what I know or the interaction between them and my website / app / product? How can I build for them a stronger, quicker, or more enjoyable experience?

In fact, what are my consumers ' actions and preferences today? Can such decisions be automated on the basis of a certain knowledge that I already have or might have?

How can I better identify good and bad experiences for customers? Can I detect problems that affect customer experience or satisfaction before they occur or spread?

New Verticals Or Customers

Do I have any data which can be useful for other industry or neighboring industry stakeholders? What kind of choices can these stakeholders make?

What are the indicators or patterns if I were to foresee accurately, might dramatically affect my ability to support my customers or otherwise perform in the market, such as predicted demand for some product categories, cost volatility, etc?

What are the key entities I collect data (people, companies, products, etc.) about? Can I marry the data with external data (from public sources, partners, etc.) in a way that tells me something new or useful about them? Who and how useful? For example: identify potential customers on the verge of seeking your products, understand how external factors affect demand in your industry, etc.

Brainstorm some of these issues (and others) with your manager and main corporate stakeholders. If you don't know where to begin — begin anywhere. You and your colleagues can only play with some data and find out where you can go from.

In the following section, we will cover all the technical terms ML that PMs need to consider, how the issue concept influences technology choice and how some of the modeling vulnerabilities that have an effect on their company.

WHAT YOU NEED TO KNOW ABOUT MACHINE LEARNING ALGORITHMS AND WHY YOU SHOULD CARE

We discussed previously the type of business impact that ML can have. Let's now review all technical terms and conditions you need to know to work with a data science team effectively and help them to have the greatest impact on your company (or at least sound like you know what they talk about).

Algorithms, models and data We are designing a computer at a design level that, given certain inputs, produces a certain desired performance by discovering and learning from trends in data.

A very typical scenario is that a computer starts by looking at a certain collection of inputs and a range of outputs that suit certain inputs. It identifies patterns and creates a set of complex rules which can be applied to new inputs not previously seen and produces the desired result. For example, we want to predict the home price (output) in view of the square images, addresses, and a number of rooms (the input). Let us assume that we have details on the square footage, the address, and the amount of the rooms and the sales price of 10,000 homes. The computer is "educated" itself on the data— i.e., it detects trends that decide how square footage, address and number of rooms affect the cost of a house and, thus, will estimate the price of the house if you send it 3 inputs for a house that it has not seen before.

The job of the data scientist is to find the optimal input and the predicted output to use. She has several templates for machines, called algorithms. The devices she creates from these designs are called concept projects to solve a certain problem. Templates have various options and configurations to produce different templates from the same design. You can use different templates and/or tweak the same template settings to generate many models that you can test to check which results will be best.

Remember that the performance of the model is right / useful to make decisions with some likelihood. The forecasts are not 100% accurate, but rather "reasonable guesses" given the amount of data seen by the algorithm. The more data the model saw, the more likely the output is to be useful.

The "training set" is the set of known inputs and outputs the data scientist uses to "train" the machine— i.e., to allow the model to identify data patterns and to establish rules. For one or more "templates," these data are used to build one or more models, which data scientists believe will help to solve the problem. Remember that even if you only use a "template" (algorithm), you can change those options to create multiple models from the same prototype and with different settings, so you actually get multiple models.

After having some of these "trained" models, she needs to check how well they work and which models work best. She uses the new data known as the "validation package." She runs the validation input models to see which results are nearest to the validation outputs. In our case, which model predicts the house price nearest to the actual price for which the house was sold. At this point, she needs a fresh set of data because the models are made on the basis of their success with the training set and are therefore inclined to work well and do not give a real lecture.

Upon validating what model is the strongest and choosing the winner, our data scientist has to assess the true performance of that model, i.e., how successful the best model she will create is really to solve the problem. Finally, she needs a new dataset because the model works specifically in the training and validation sets–this is how it was chosen! The last set of data is classified as the "check sample." In our case, she must check how similar the expected prices for the test set inputs are to the checked domestic prices. We will discuss performance measurement later in more detail.

Some Popular "Buzzwords" Worth Knowing There are some other words that you often encounter when operating in space. The connection (or lack of) to the groups we spoke about is important to understand.

Deep learning is orthogonal to the definitions mentioned above. It is just the application of a particular type of system to solve learning problems— the solution can be monitored, unchecked, etc.

An artificial neural network (ANN) is a learning system which simulates the workings of our brain — by means of a network of layered "neurons." A neural network has at least one input layer— a group of neurons that integrate data into the network, an output layer — neurons through which the effects are transmitted, and one or more layers above them, which are considered "secret layers," the layers that do the calculations. Deep learning is simply the utilization of neural networks with more than one hidden layer to perform a learning task. If you ever use these networks-congratulations, you can also honestly chuck around the mouthpiece!

Ensemble methods or ensemble learning are the use of multiple models in order to achieve a result that is better than each individual model can achieve. The models may be based on different algorithms or different parameters on a single algorithm. The theory is that instead of providing a model that uses input and outputs output — say some form of the forecast; you have a series of models that each create a prediction and a method to compare different outcomes and determine what the performance of the system is to be. Methods of the combination are often used in supervised learning (they are very useful for problem prediction) but can also be used in unattended learning. Your data science team will probably test and apply these methods where necessary.

The field of computer science dealing with language understanding by machines is natural language processing (NLP). Machine learning is not used by all forms of NLP. For starters, a "verb cloud"— a visual representation of the number of times the term occurs in a document — does not require understanding. More sophisticated research and language and document interpretation also involve ML. Some examples: generation of keywords. Understand the topic of a body of text and create keywords for it automatically Language confusion. Determining the specific meaning of multiple possible meanings of a phrase or a sentence (for example, this is a great explanation). Considering where the emotion conveyed in a text is on the basis of negative to positive lies Extraction of the individual. Business, individuals, places, products, etc. are defined in a text, particularly challenging if the names are not identifiable (for example, the company "Microsoft" is easier to identify than the company "Target," also in the English-language word). It is also commonly used for planning and pre-processing data until it can provide useful input into many ML models. Details later on.

Please note: the above meanings express the main ideas and are practical; refer to other references for a comprehensive scientific definition.

How The Problem Affects The Solution (And Some More Key ML Concepts)

Many downstream decisions will dictate the strategic objective that you are trying to achieve with ML. In order to ensure your data science team can provide the right solution for your company, it is important to understand some simple ML principles and their effect on your business goals.

Algorithm selection

A small change in the problem definition can mean that a completely different algorithm is required to resolve this problem, or at least a different model with different data inputs will be created. A platform that tries to classify types of photos that fit well for people can use unsupervised learning techniques, such as clustering, to recognize similar subjects, while the challenge with suggesting potential dates for a specific person is that the system can use supervised learning based on inputs that are unique to the particular user, such as the photos it already looks at.

Feature selection

ML selection models identify data patterns. The details you apply to the models are grouped into properties (also known as variables or attributes): These are important, largely independent data objects that explain some characteristics of the phenomena you are attempting to predict or define.

Consider the previous example of an organization that wants to give preference to loan borrowers. If we define the problem as "prioritizing customers on their chance to convert," we include characteristics such as the response rate of similar customers to the various types of services provided by the company. When we define the problem as "prioritize consumers to pay back their debt," then these attributes may not be included because they are not applicable to the estimation of the possibility of reimbursement by customers.

Objective function selection

The aim of the method is to compensate for or to forecast the outcome of the experiment. For instance, if you try to suggest items for which a consumer may be interesting, the performance of a model could be the possibility that if the user sees the product, he clicks on it. It may also be possible that the consumer would buy the drug. The choosing of the objective feature is primarily a function of your market target— you are more involved in user engagement here, in which case the objective role may be clicked, or time spent, or a direct profit. The other important consideration is the availability of the data: to learn the algorithm, you must feed many data points that have been "labeled" positively (the products that a user has seen and clicked on) or negatively (the products which a user has seen and not clicked on). You may have more data points of products clicked (or not clicked) compared to products bought in order of magnitude.

Explanation and interpretability

The performance of ML models is often counted— the likelihood that something occurs or is real is expected. In the example of the product recommendations, the products on the website are likely to be clicked by an individual customer, and the products with the highest probability are shown to the user. But how do you think it's functioning? In this case, it is relatively easy to check that the algorithm works — you may run a quick test and see. But what if the rating individuals are future hires and your concept shows that they are likely to be good client candidates? Will, a user (say, a hiring manager) just take your word or understand why the algorithm ranks A in front of person B?

In many situations, you have something to say. Many ML algorithms are a black box; however: you enter many features and get a model that is hard to understand. The trends identified by the algorithm in the data are often so complex that even if they are easy to put in English, a person can not understand them.

In the following sections, we will find that the need for explanation–to what extent the end-user needs to be able to understand how the result is achieved and the level of interpretability-is critical to how far the user needs to draw certain findings based on the results.

Modeling And Performance Measurement Pitfalls Pms Should Watch Out For

Your data scientists will deal with some common issues with data processing and modeling, but it is useful for PMs to understand some common pitfalls in order to engage in productive discussions. This is not an exhaustive list, but it contains some of the most common problems.

Overfitting

A model is said to be' overfitted' by closely following the data to describe too much of the noise than the real underlying relationship within the data (see illustration). If the model's accuracy on the data with which you practice (data from which the model "learns") is significantly better than its accuracy on the data with which you verify and check it, you may have an overfit.

Precision, Recall and the Tradeoff Between Them

Two words are very vague when you first encounter them, but they are important to understand because they have clear business ramifications.

Precision and recall are often calculated by two key metrics: the precision of the assignment (and other commonly employed ML strategies like the record recovery). Precision tests the share of real positive predictions out of all the good predictions made by the algorithm, i.e., the percentages of good predictions. When the accuracy is X%, X% of the positive forecasts of the algorithm are true positive and (100-X)% are false positive. The greater the performance, the less false positives you will have.

Note the share of optimistic forecasts from all the true positive data—i.e., what% of the true positive data the algorithm has classified as good. When the warning reaches X percent, the algorithm classified X percent of the true positives in the data as valid when (100-X) percent are defined as (fake) negatives. In other words, the higher the more false negatives you will remember.

There is always a balance between consistency and warning. If you do not want false positive— i.e., you require greater precision, the algorithm will have more false negatives, i.e., a lower warning, as "prefer" to mark something as wrong than negatively, or vice versa. This arrangement is a business decision. Take the example: if you'd like to play it wisely and only admit applicants you are certain you want to approve, this increases the chance of denying any good customers (more specificity, fewer reminder= less false positive, more false negative) or of approving more loan applicants who should be denied but who don't risk good customers failing (greater reminder but lower p Although this can be said to be a question of optimization, there are often variables that are not easily quantifiable, such as the customer's perception (i.e., consumers who are unjustly rejected become fed up and vocal), brand danger (e.g., the credibility as a lender relies on a low loan default rate), legal obligations etc.

The Often Misleading Model Accuracy Metric

For any sample, model consistency alone is not a good measure. Picture an illness with a community prevalence of 0.1 percent. A model which says no patient is 99.9 percent correct, but completely unnecessary, irrespective of the data. It is important that both precision and recall are always taken into consideration and balanced according to business needs. Exactness is a good measure when the distribution of possible outcomes is quite consistent, and the importance of false positive and false negatives, which is rarely the case, is also equal.

Averaging Metrics and Imbalanced Training Data

When dealing with multiple segments of the model, you have to look separately at the performance metrics for each segment (or at least the important segments). Take a classification model, for instance, that classifies pictures in one of the categories by animal type in the photo. The overall accuracy / recall number of the model may not be a situation in which some categories have high accuracy, while others have low accuracy. This is often when the teaching data becomes imbalanced-say. You have 1,000 labeled pictures of cats and dogs and only 10 pictures of bears. Your total accuracy may be very good because most of the pictures of the cats and the dogs are correctly labeled, while all bears are incorrectly categorized as the model has little or no details. If these less common types are essential for your company, a concerted effort may be required to obtain training information to make the pattern function across the board.

Sure — it's been pretty long, so ideally, you already learn all the technological basics. First, we should observe the comprehensive step-by-step process of developing a concept from ideation to development start.

MACHINE LEARNING MODELS

A deep dive into and use the various machine learning models! First of all, we talked about the part art, part science, of selecting the perfect model for learning a machine.

Eventually, we dive deeper into the different virtual learning devices you can train and use!

Tree-based models generally perform best in Kaggle competitions. The other models are great assembly candidates. CNN's outperform everything for computer vision challenges. LSTMs or GRUs are your best bet for natural language processing!

Here is a non-exhaustive laundry list of models to be tried and some context for each model.

Regression

Regression → Linear Regression → Vanilla Linear Regression

Benefits

Records linear relationships in the dataset well

If you have a couple of well-defined variables and require a basic predictive design, Works well

Quick training speed and forecast speeds

Succeeds on little datasets

Interpretable outcomes, simple to describe

Easy to update the model when brand-new data comes in

No specification tuning required (the regularized linear designs listed below need to tune the regularization criterion).

It does not need feature scaling (the regularized direct designs below requirement function scaling).

If the dataset has redundant features, direct regression can be unstable.

Downsides.

It does not work well for non-linear data.

Low(er) prediction accuracy.

Can overfit (see regularized models listed below to counteract this).

Doesn't a different signal from noise well-- cull unimportant features prior to usage.

It doesn't discover function interactions in the dataset.

Regression → Linear Regression → Lasso, Ridge, Elastic-Net Regression

Benefits

These designs are direct regression with regularization

Assist combat overfitting

Since they are simpler, these models are much better at generalizing

When we only care about a few features, they work well

Downsides

Required function scaling

Required to tune the regularization criterion

Regression → Regression Trees → Decision Tree

Benefits

Fast training speed and prediction speeds

Records non-linear relationships in the dataset well

Learns function interactions in the dataset

When your dataset has outliers, Great

Great for discovering the essential features in the dataset

Doesn't require feature scaling

Decently interpretable outcomes, simple to discuss

Drawbacks

Low(er) prediction precision

Requires some specification tuning

Does not succeed on small datasets

Does not differentiate signal from sound well

When brand-new data comes in, not simply to upgrade the model

Used really rarely in practice, use ensembled trees rather

Can overfit (see ensembled designs listed below).

Regression → Regression Trees → Ensembles

Benefits

Collates forecasts from numerous trees

High prediction precision-- does actually well in practice

Preferred algorithm in Kaggle competitors

Great when your dataset has outliers

Records non-linear relationships in the dataset well

Great for discovering the essential functions in the dataset

Separates signal vs. noise

Does not need feature scaling

Perform actually well on high-dimensional information

Drawbacks

Slower training speed

Fast forecast speed

Difficult to discuss or analyze

When new data comes in, not easy to update the model

Requires some specification tuning-- Harder to tune

Does not succeed on little datasets

Regression → Deep Learning

Benefits

High prediction accuracy-- does actually well in practice

Captures very complicated underlying patterns in the data

Does truly well with both huge datasets and those with high-dimensional information

Easy to upgrade the design when new information comes in

The network's hidden layers minimize the requirement for feature engineering extremely

Is state of the art for computer vision, device translation, belief analysis, and speech recognition jobs

Downsides

Long training speed

Required a huge amount of computing power

Need function scaling

Challenging to describe or analyze results

Since it discovers a vast number of criteria, required lots of training information

Surpassed by Boosting algorithms for non-image, non-text, non-speech jobs

Really versatile, featured lots of different architecture foundation, thus require proficiency to create the architecture

Regression → K Nearest Neighbors (Distance Based)

Benefits

Fast training speed

Doesn't need much specification tuning

Interpretable results, easy to discuss

Works well for little datasets (< 100k training set).

Drawbacks.

Low(er) prediction precision.

It doesn't succeed on little datasets.

Need to pick a suitable range function.

Requirements feature scaling to work well.

Forecast speed grows with the size of the dataset.

Does not differentiate signal from noise well-- cull unimportant features prior to usage.

Since it conserves every observation, it is memory intensive.

Likewise means they do not work well with high-dimensional information.

2. Classification

Classification → Logistic Regression

Benefits

Classifies linearly separable information well

Quick training speed and forecast speeds

Succeeds on small datasets

Decently interpretable outcomes, easy to explain

Easy to upgrade the model when brand-new data can be found in

When regularized, can prevent overfitting

Can do both 2 class and multiclass classification

No specification tuning required (other than when regularized, we require to tune the regularization specification).

When regularized), it does not require function scaling (except.

If the dataset has redundant functions, direct regression can be unsteady.

Downsides.

It doesn't work well for non-linearly separable data.

Low(er) forecast accuracy.

Can overfit (see regularized models listed below).

Doesn't a separate signal from sound well-- cull irrelevant functions before use.

It does not learn feature interactions in the dataset.

Classification → Support Vector Machines (Distance-based)

Benefits

High prediction precision

Doesn't overfit, even on high-dimensional datasets, so it's terrific for when you have lots of features

Functions well for little datasets (< 100k training set).

Work well for text category issues.

Drawbacks.

Not easy to update the design when new information comes in.

Is it very memory intensive?

It does not work well on big datasets.

When new data comes in, not easy to update the design.

Needs you choose the right kernel in order to work.

The direct kernel designs direct data and works quickly.

The non-linear kernels can model non-linear limits and can be slow.

Usage Boosting rather!

Classification → Naive Bayes (Probability-based)

Benefits

Carries out actually well on text classification problems

Fast training speed and prediction speeds

Succeeds on little datasets

Separates signal from sound well

Carries out well in practice

Basic, easy to implement

Functions well for little datasets (< 100k training set).

The ignorant assumption about the self-reliance of functions and their potential circulation lets it avoid overfitting.

Likewise, if this condition of independence holds, Naive Bayes can work on smaller sized datasets and can have much faster training speed.

It does not need feature scaling.

Not memory extensive.

Decently interpretable results, easy to describe.

Scales well with the size of the dataset.

Drawbacks.

Low(er) prediction accuracy.

Classification → K Nearest Neighbors (Distance Based)

Benefits

Quick training speed

Doesn't require much criterion tuning

Interpretable outcomes, easy to discuss

Works well for small datasets (< 100k training set).

Drawbacks.

Low(er) prediction precision.

It does not succeed in small datasets.

Need to pick an ideal range function.

Requirements include scaling to work well.

Forecast speed grows with the size of the dataset.

Doesn't a separate signal from sound well-- cull irrelevant features before usage.

Is memory extensive due to the fact that it conserves every observation.

Likewise indicates they don't work well with high-dimensional data.

Classification → Classification Tree → Decision Tree

Benefits

Fast training speed and prediction speeds

Catches non-linear relationships in the dataset well

Learns function interactions in the dataset

When your dataset has outliers, Great

Great for finding the essential features in the dataset

Can do both 2 class and multiclass classification

Doesn't require feature scaling

Decently interpretable outcomes, easy to discuss

Drawbacks

Low(er) forecast precision

Needs some criterion tuning

Does not succeed on small datasets

Doesn't a different signal from sound well

Used extremely hardly ever in practice, use ensembled trees instead

When brand-new data comes in, not simply to update the model

Can overfit (see ensembled models below).

Classification → Classification Tree → Ensembles

Benefits

Collects forecasts from numerous trees

High prediction accuracy-- does truly well in practice

The preferred algorithm in Kaggle competitions

Catches non-linear relationships in the dataset well

Great when your dataset has outliers

Great for discovering the most important functions in the dataset

Separates signal vs. noise

Doesn't need function scaling

Perform really well on high-dimensional data

Drawbacks

Slower training speed

Quick prediction speed

Hard to explain or interpret

When brand-new information comes in, not simply to upgrade the model

Needs some parameter tuning-- Harder to tune

Doesn't succeed on little datasets

Classification → Deep Learning

Benefits

High prediction precision-- does truly well in practice

Records very intricate underlying patterns in the information

Does really well with both big datasets and those with high-dimensional information

When new information comes in, Easy to upgrade the design

The network's covert layers reduce the need for function engineering incredibly

Is cutting-edge for computer system vision, maker translation, belief analysis, and speech recognition jobs

Drawbacks

Long training speed

Difficult to describe or interpret results

Need a big amount of computing power

Required function scaling

Required lots of training information since it learns a vast number of parameters

Outperformed by Boosting algorithms for non-image, non-text, non-speech tasks

Really versatile, included great deals of different architecture building blocks, therefore require expertise to create the architecture

3. Clustering

Clustering → DBSCAN

Benefits

Scalable to large datasets

Detects sound well

Don't need to know the number of clusters ahead of time

Does not make an assumption that the shape of the cluster is globular

Drawbacks

Does not always work if your entire dataset is densely loaded

Need to tune the density specifications-- epsilon and min_samples to the best values to get good results

Clustering → KMeans

Benefits

Great for revealing the structure of the underlying dataset

Basic, simple to interpret

Works well if you know the number of clusters in advance

Drawbacks

Does not constantly work if your clusters aren't globular and similar in size

Requirements to understand the number of clusters in advance-- Required to tune the option of k clusters to get great results

Memory extensive

Does not scale to big datasets

4. Misc — Models not included here

Dimensionality Reduction Algorithms

Clustering algorithms — Gaussian Mixture Model and Hierarchical clustering

Computer Vision — Convolutional Neural Networks, Image classification, Object Detection, Image segmentation

Natural Language Processing — RNNs (LSTM or GRUs)

Reinforcement Learning

Ensembling Your Models

Mounting models is a very effective approach that eliminates overfitting and allows accurate predictions by integrating outputs from various models. It is a crucial tool for winning Kaggle competitions in particular.

When we collect models to combine, we want to choose them from various model classes to make sure that they have different strengths and weaknesses and therefore capture different patterns in the data set. This greater diversity leads to lower partialities. They also want to ensure that their efficiency is equal to maintain the accuracy of the forecasts.

In fact, the mixing of these models led to much lower losses than any one model could produce alone. Part of the reason is that while these models are all very effective at forecasting, they have specific predictions, and we are able to combine all their different strengths into a super-powerful model by merging them.

There are 4 types of ensembling (including blending):

Bagging: Train several base models with different, randomly selected data subsets and substitute them. Let the basic models vote on final forecasts. In RandomForests. Using.

Boosting: Train models and update the importance of getting each example right after every iteration. Used in the GradientBoosting program.

Blending: Practice different regression models and render holdout predictions. Train a new model from its predictions to predict the test set. (A holdout package stacking).

Stack: Train several forms of basic models and simulate k-folds of the data set. Stacking: Train a new model from its predictions to predict the test set.

Comparing weights and biases models allows you to track and compare model performance with a line of code.

Once you have selected a configuration, you want to use, train and simply add wandb.log to log your model condition.({' score': cv score}). You can compare your model performance on an easy dashboard once you have completed your training!

WandB

import wandb

```python
import tensorflow.keras

from wandb.keras import WandbCallback

from sklearn.model_selection import cross_val_score

# Import models (Step 1: add your models here)

from sklearn import svm

from sklearn.linear_model import Ridge, RidgeCV

from xgboost import XGBRegressor



# Model 1

# Initialize wandb run

#You can change here the name of your project. See more configuration
options https://docs.wandb.com/docs/init.html

wandb.init(anonymous='allow', project="pick-a-model")



# Initialize model (Step 2: add your classifier here)

clf = svm.SVR(C= 20, epsilon= 0.008, gamma=0.0003)
```

```
# Get CV scores

cv_scores = cross_val_score(clf, X_train, train_labels, cv=5)



# Log scores

for cv_score in cv_scores:

    wandb.log({'score': cv_score})



# Model 2

# Initialize wandb run

# You can change your project name here. For more config options, see
https://docs.wandb.com/docs/init.html

wandb.init(anonymous='allow', project="pick-a-model")



# Initialize model (Step 2: add your classifier here)

clf = XGBRegressor(learning_rate=0.01,

  n_estimators=6000,

  max_depth=4,
```

```
        min_child_weight=0,

        gamma=0.6,

        subsample=0.7,

        colsample_bytree=0.7,

        objective='reg:linear',

        nthread=-1,

        scale_pos_weight=1,

        seed=27,

        reg_alpha=0.00006,

        random_state=42)


# Get CV scores

cv_scores = cross_val_score(clf, X_train, train_labels, cv=5)


# Log scores

for cv_score in cv_scores:

    wandb.log({'score': cv_score})
```

Model 3

Initialize wandb run

You can change your project name here. For more config options, see https://docs.wandb.com/docs/init.html

wandb.init(anonymous='allow', project="pick-a-model")

Initialize model (Step 2: add your classifier here)

ridge_alphas = [1e-15, 1e-10, 1e-8, 9e-4, 7e-4, 5e-4, 3e-4, 1e-4, 1e-3, 5e-2, 1e-2, 0.1, 0.3, 1, 3, 5, 10, 15, 18, 20, 30, 50, 75, 100]

clf = Ridge(alphas=ridge_alphas)

Get CV scores

cv_scores = cross_val_score(clf, X_train, train_labels, cv=5)

Log scores

for cv_score in cv_scores:

   wandb.log({'score': cv_score})

DEVELOPING A MACHINE LEARNING MODEL FROM START TO FINISH

You will learn all the basic principles so that we can now transform an idea into a real model of development.

Modeling at glance

At a high level, the creation of a good ML model is like the creation of any other product: You start with the idea where you align yourself with the problem you want to solve and with a few potential approaches. Once the path is simple, you build the plan and check it to see if it meets your needs. You continue to iterate between ideas, prototyping, and testing until your solution is good enough to bring it into the market. Now let's dig into each stage's info.

Since data is an integral part of ML, we need to put data on top of this development process, so our new process looks like this:

Ideation. Align with the key problem to be addressed and the potential data sources to be taken into account.

Preparation of data. Collect and obtain data in a useful format to digest and learn from a model.

Testing and prototyping. Create a model or series of models to solve the problem, check their output, and iterate until you have a model with a satisfactory result.

Productization. Stabilize and scale your plan, capture, and analyze your data to produce useful outcomes in your production environment.

Ideation

The aim of this process is to work together as a team to resolve the key problem posed by the concept, its target function, and its possible inputs.

Align yourself with the issue. Machine learning, as mentioned, must be used to address a real business problem. Ensure that all the people on your staff and the organization decide on the issue and how you are going to use the remedy.

Choose an impartial function. Decide, depending on the question, what the model's goal should be. Does the model attempt to predict an objective function? Is there a metric of "fact," to which you can test "land facts" results, including home prices, increase in stock prices, etc.?? Instead, are you only trying to find data patterns? For example, group pictures into groups with something in common?

Define metrics of consistency. How would you measure the quality of the model? Sometimes it is difficult to predict what optimal output is without seeing the outcomes, but a guiding understanding of the target is beneficial.

Potential sources to brainstorm. Your goal is to determine which data can assist you in solving the problem / taking decisions. The most helpful query is: "How would a space specialist deal with this problem?"Think about the variables / data pieces on which the individual would base a solution. Any aspect that could affect human judgment should be tested— as wide as possible at this point — knowing the key factors that require issue awareness of the business space, which is one of the reasons why it's necessary to include companies / products at this point. These potential inputs must be translated into model features by the data team. Please note that additional processing may be required to convert inputs into functions— more on that next.

Data Preparation

The aim is to collect raw data and to enter it into a form that can be connected to your prototype model as an input. To do this, you may need to perform complicated transformations on the results. Suppose, for example, that a customer sentiment about a company is one of your features: you must first find appropriate outlets when customers think about the item. When the brand name contains widely known terms (e.g.,' Apple'), you have to distinguish the brand chatter from the general chatter (on the fruit) and use the sentiment analysis model before starting constructing the prototype. Not all apps are so difficult to create, but some might require a lot of effort.

Let's take a closer look at this stage:

Collect data for your project as fast as possible. Identify your missing data first. In some cases, you might have to break down the inputs necessary to reach the level of raw data "building blocks," which is more easily available, or the data which is close to what you need, and which is easier to get. Consider the fastest and easiest way to get your details once you have found it. Non-scalable procedures such as a fast manual update, a simple scraper or a review of knowledge, even if the most practical approach is a little cost-effective. It typically makes no sense to spend too much in increasing the database creation now because you do not know how valuable the data would be, which format it would be better, and so on. Business people should be interested — they will also explore opportunities to find data that is not available easily or just collect it for the team (relevant business functions rely on the data needs and the company framework—alliances, management innovations or promotions can support here). Remember that you do not just need knowledge for model features in the case of a supervised learning algorithm; you need so-called' ground reality ' data points for the objective purpose of your model, to train and then validate and check your model. Returning to the example of home prices–you need to view several homes with prices to build a model that forecasts home prices!

Cleaning and normalizing results. At this stage, the data science / engineering team is largely responsible. There is important research in converting concepts and raw data sets into actual model inputs. Data sets should be reviewed and cleaned to avoid abuse of information, invalid outliers, etc. For order to work with or fit with other data sets, it may need to be converted into a different scale. Especially when dealing with text and images, the pre-treatment of the data is usually necessary to retrieve the relevant information. If, for example, too many big images are plugged into a model, a huge amount of information may not be processable so you can lower quality, work with part of the image or use only object outlines. In the case of language, you may have to identify the people that are important to you in the document before agreeing to include it, execute a nostalgic evaluation, find common n-grams (often used word sequences) or create several other transformations. These are generally supported by current repositories that need no reinventing of the wheel by the staff, but take time.

Prototyping And Testing

The goal of this process is to enter, evaluate, and iterate a prototype of a concept before you come to a model that provides sufficient performance to be ready for production.

Build a template. The data science department will start working on the actual model once the data is in good form. Bear in mind that at this point, there is a lot of art in research. There are many tests and developments involved–a collection of the most important elements, various algorithms, etc. It is not always an easy task, and the timetable of achieving a successful pattern can, therefore, be very uncertain. There are situations in which the first algorithm evaluated yields great results and where nothing performs well.

Prototype evaluation and checking. At this point, the data scientists must take measures to ensure that the final model is as strong as it can be. They evaluate the model performance on the basis of the predefined quality measurements, compare different algorithms they tried, adjust any parameters which influence the performance of the model, and finally evaluate the final model's performance. For supervised learning, they will need to assess whether the model's forecasts are strong enough for the purposes in accordance with the simple reality results. For unregulated learning, depending on the issue, there are different strategies for evaluating efficiency. That said, there are many issues where it helps a lot to just look at the results. For example, when clustering, you can easily plot the objects you cluster in different dimensions or even consume objects that are a media form to see whether the clustering is intuitively reasonable. If your algorithm marks keyword papers, are the keywords meaningful? Does tagging fail, or are important uses missing? There are glaring gaps? This does not replace more scientific methods, but in practice, it helps to identify improvements quickly. This is also an environment that requires another pair of eyes, so don't just save it for the data science department.

Iterate. Iterate. You will discuss with your team at this point what more iterations are needed. How does the model compare with your expectations? Does it work well enough to improve the company's current situation significantly? Are there places in which it is especially weak? Is it appropriate to have a larger number of data points? May you think about additional performance features? Does the quality of the model's inputs have alternative data sources? Etc. Etc. Further brainstorming is often required here.

Productization

You get to this point as you conclude that your test model works fairly well to begin with and to start production. Remember that, if you're not willing to commit to full production, you need to find out which measurements you want your model to scale first. If your software is a movie recommendation tool: you can only want to open access to a number of users but provide each user a complete experience, in which case each movie in your database needs to be rated according to consumer relevance. This is another collection of scalable criteria than to make recommendations for action films but to open up exposure to all apps.

Now let's think about the more technical aspects of model production: rising data coverage. In many cases, you prototype your model based on a smaller data set than in the production process. For starters, you test the concept on a specific consumer segment and must then apply it to your whole customer base.

Size a set of info. After you have checked which data is usable for the application, you will build a reliable way of collecting and ingesting data. During the prototype stage, it was all right to collect data manually and ad-hoc, but you want to simplify this as much as possible for output.

Update info. Refresh data. Establish a time-consuming process that changes current principles or adds new knowledge. Besides having to keep historical data, the program needs a way to store increasing amounts of data over time.

Models size. It has a data science as well as an engineering dimension. When you change the underlying details from the data science viewpoint, e.g., increase the percentages of consumer groups, you will retrain and re-test the models. A paradigm that fits well on a particular data set will not always operate on a broader or separate data set. Architecturally, the architecture needs to be able to scale up to increasing quantities of data more regularly. In the example of the movie recommendations, more users, more movies and more information about the preferences of each user will probably be available over time.

Outliers search. Although the model as a whole can scale very well, small but significant communities can not fit well for the model. Of instance, your film suggestions will function well for consumers on average, but mostly children's movies will be shown for parents when they pick movies on their children's accounts. This is a product design issue— you need to distinguish the parent's suggestions from the product's children's guidance, but the layout won't say it.

What I have already mentioned is a logical flood. In fact, the lines always merge, and between phases, you need to go back and forth quite often. You may get unsatisfactory outcomes from your data collection activities and have to rethink or produce the sample to ensure the production data performs so badly that you have to go back to prototyping etc.

A Note on Outsourcing

Modeling also requires certain time-consuming and Sisyphus processes, such as creating labeled data and model checking. For example, marking hundreds or thousands of data points for an algorithm input with the right categories and verifying whether the performance of the classification model is accurate. It is very helpful to develop an on-demand system to outsource activities when they occur. In my experience, you can get decent results from Mechanical Turkish if you get many people to do the same simple task and take the more regular or average answer. There are services such as CrowdFlower, which provide more reliable results, but also cost more. Many tasks require further pre-training for the persons who conduct it (e.g., if the job is space sensitive and/or needs previous information), where you may want to search sites such as Upwork.

INTRODUCTION TO NEURAL NETWORKS FOR MACHINE LEARNING

Neural networks are a concept type within the overall literature of the computer. Neural networks are a particular set of machine learning algorithms. They are inspired by biological neural networks, and the current so-called deep neural networks have worked very well. Neural networks are general estimations of functions themselves, which is why they can be used to learn virtually any computer question by performing a complicated mapping from the input to the output space.

Three factors to research the neural computation are: to learn how the brain works: it's very big and very complex, and it's constructed from a material that dies while you stay with it, so we need to use computer simulations.

Please grasp a neuron-inspired form of parallel calculation and its adaptive connections: it is a very different style of series calculation.

To solve practical difficulties by using new brain-inspired learning algorithms, learning algorithms can be very helpful even if they don't work in the brain.

Top 10 architecture of the neural network you need to learn

1-Perceptrons

Considered to be the first type of neuronal cells, they are essentially computer models of a single neuron. Frank Rosenblatt invented Perceptron ("The perceptron: a probabilistic paradigm for brain-based information storage and organization"). Often known as the neural feed-forward network, a perceptron provides information from the front to the back. Learning perceptrons usually require back-propagation, supplying inputs and outputs in-network paired datasets. Inputs are sent to the neuron, interpreted, and generated. Usually, the error reported back is the difference between the input and output data. If the network has enough secret neurons, the interaction between input and output can always be modeled. For reality, they are much narrower in use but are often merged with other networks to form new networks.

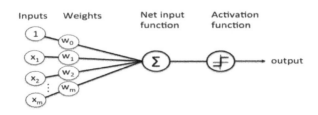

Schematic of Rosenblatt's perceptron.

When you pick and have enough apps by hand, you can do almost anything. With binary input vectors, we can have an infinitely large number of binary vectors with a different function unit and can allow some conceivable prejudice against binary input vectors. There are, however, drawbacks to perceptrons: once the hand-coded characteristics are established, there are extremely strong limits on what a perceptron can know.

2 - Convolutional Neural Networks

In 1998, Yann LeCun and his colleagues created a very strong LeNet recognizer for handwritten numbers. It used backpropagation within a feedforward network with a large number of caching layers, many mappings of replicated units in each layer, output pooling of nearby replicated units, a broad network that can handle several characters at once, even when they overlap, and a smart way to train a whole system, not just a recognizor. Later it was officially named*** convolutional neural networks (CNNs)***.

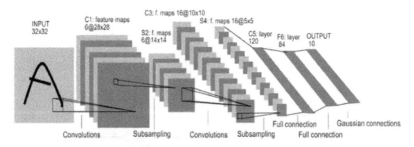

Fig. 2. Architecture of LeNet-5, a Convolutional Neural Network, here for digits recognition. Each plane is a feature map, i.e. a set of units whose weights are constrained to be identical.

The neural networks in Convolution are quite distinct from most other networks. These are primarily used for the encoding of photographs but can also be used for other data forms such as audio. A typical example of use with CNNs is where network photos are fed, and details are categorized. CNN's tend to start with the "scanner" input which does not attempt to decode all training data simultaneously. For example, you don't want a layer with 10,000 nodes to enter an image of 100x 100 pixels. Alternatively, a scanning input layer of say 10x10 is generated and the first 10x10 picture is fed. When this information is transferred, you must feed the scanner for the next 10x 10 pixels by pushing the scanner to the right.

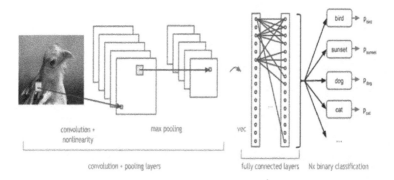

This data is then fed through convolutional layers, not regular layers, in which not all nodes are linked. That node is concerned only with adjacent cells. Such convolutional layers often tend to decline as they get thicker, primarily by quickly separating input factors. In addition to these convolutional structures, they also often have pooling layers. Pooling is a way of filtering out details: a common technique for pooling is max pooling in which we take, say, 2x 2 pixels, and move on a red pixel. Read Yann LeCun's initial article, "Gradient-based learning for text comprehension" (1998), if you are to delve more thoroughly into CNNs.

3–Recurrent neural networks

We need a brief overview of sequence modeling to understand RNNs. We often want to turn an input sequence into an output sequence that lives in a different area while applying machine learning to sequences. For example, transform a sound pressure series into a sequence of word identities. If we don't have a specific target list, a teaching signal can be obtained by anticipating the next word in the input sequence. The goal output sequence is a one-step input series. It seems to be much more normal than projecting one pixel in a frame or a part of an image in the rest of the photo. The estimation in a series of the next word blurs the difference between controlled and unattended instruction. This employs approaches intended for guided study but does not require a separate trigger for training.

The standard approach to this task is memoryless models. In particular self-repressive models can predict a sequence of previous terms using "delay taps" for the next term. Neural feed-forward networks are generalized self-representing models that use one or more layers of non-linear hidden units. If, however, our generative model is hidden and if we give its internal dynamics to this hidden state, we get a much interesting model that can store information for a long time in its hidden state. If the mechanics and how they produce outputs from their hidden state are running, we will never know their exact hidden state. The best we can do is deduce a distribution of probabilities across the field of hidden state vectors. This is only true with two forms of hidden state models.

Recurring neural networks (RNNs) were mainly perceptrons originally introduced in Jeffrey Elman's "Seeing meaning in time" (1990). But as compared to stateless perceptrons, they provide relations between passes and interactions over time. RNNs are very effective as they incorporate two features: 1) a global, secret status, which enables you to store a lot of past knowledge effectively, and 2) non-linear dynamics, allowing you to change the hidden state in complicated ways. RNNs can simulate everything the machine can measure with enough neurons and time. So what type of behavior will RNNs show? They can oscillate, settle down, and behave chaotically. You can learn how to execute several small programs, each of which catches and runs simultaneously to achieve very complicated results.

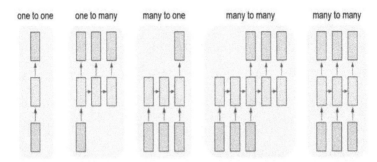

one to one   one to many   many to one   many to many   many to many

One major problem for RNNs is the fluttering (or exploding) gradient problem, where information is lost quickly over time, depending on the activation functions used. This would not be an intuitive problem because these are only weights and not neuron states, but the time weights actually store past information. If the weight is 0 or 1000,000,000, the previous state is not very informative. In general, RNNs can be used in many areas, since most data sources that do not really have a timeline (non-audio or video) can be interpreted as a sequence. One pixel or character at a time can be fed a picture or a text string, and time-dependent weights are not used for what was achieved seconds before in the series. Typically, recurrent networks are a successful way to advance or complete knowledge, such as autocompletion.

4-Long / Short Term Memory

Hochreiter & Schmidhuber (1997) solved the problem by constructing what are referred to as*** Long-term memory networks (LSTMs) *** to remember the long-term memory. LSTMs aims to tackle the degradation / explosion issue by adding gates and a specifically specified memory cell. The memory cell retains and holds the previous values unless a "forget gate" asks the cell to forget certain values. LSTMs also have an "input gate," which adds new items to the cell and an "exit gate," which determines how the vectors are transferred from the cell to the next secret state.

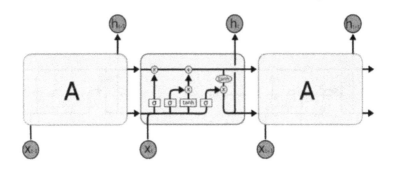

Note that with all RNNs, the X train and H previous values are used to determine what happens in the new secret condition. The current hidden condition (H current) results are used to determine what happens in the next hidden state. LSTMs simply add a cell layer to ensure that hidden state information transfer is fairly high from one iteration to the next. In another context, we want to remember things from previous iterations as long as necessary, and the LSTM cells allow this to happen. LSTMs may study complicated pieces, such as the writing of Hemingway or Mozart's composition.

5-Gated Recurrent Unit

Recurrent Gated units (GPUs) show a slight variation on the LSTMs. X train and H previous are used as inputs. They carry out certain equations and then pass H current. For further calculations, X train.next and H current are used in the next iteration. What separates them from LSTM is that GRUs do not have to transfer values through the cell sheet. The equations in each iteration guarantee that the H current values transferred either keep a lot of old information or jump-start with a lot of new information.

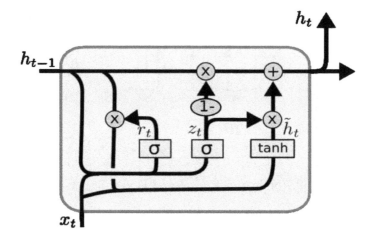

GRUs work in most cases similar to LSTMs, the biggest difference being that GRUs are slightly faster and easier to operate (but also somewhat less expressive). In practice, these tend to cancel each other, as you need a larger network to regain expressiveness, which then cancels the advantages of performance. In some situations, GRUs can surpass LSTMs if extra expressiveness is not necessary. In the 2014 "Empirical assessment of gated recurrent neural networks on sequence representation," you can learn more on GRUs.

6-Hopfield Network

Non-linear networks are typically very difficult to analyze. We will behave in many different ways: settle down to a stable state, oscillate, or take unpredictable directions that can not be predicted far into the future. In his 1982 paper "Neural networks and physical systems with emerging collective computational capabilities," John Hopfield introduced the Hopfield Net to solve this problem. The Hopfield (HN) network is a network that links all neurons to each other's neurons. It's an all-embroidered piece of pasta, as all the nodes function. Each node is input before training and ultimately concealed through exercise and training. The networks are conditioned by adjusting the neuron size to the target pattern and measuring weights. After that, the weights do not shift. The network will always converge on one of the learned patterns when trained for one or more patterns because only in these states is the network stable.

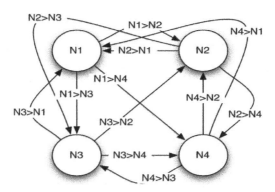

Hopfield networks have another computational function. Instead of using the net to preserve experiences, we use it to create sensory feedback interpretations. The feedback comprises of the obvious units, the circumstances of the secret units, and electricity is the bad interpretation.

Unfortunately, people have shown that the capacity of a Hopfield network is very limited. An N-Unit Hopfield Net can only memorize 0.15N patterns owing to the so-called bogus energy minima. Since the energy feature is constant over its weights, if two local minimum values are too similar, they will "break" into each other to create a single local minimum that does not suit either training sample, thus ignoring the two samples they are to hold. The amount of tests that a Hopfield system can acquire is greatly reduced by this phenomenon.

7–Boltzmann System

A Boltzmann is a kind of repeated stochastic neural network. It is known as Hopfield's stochastic, generative equivalent. It was one of the first neural networks that could learn internal representations and solve difficult combinatory problems. The Boltzmann machines were first presented by Geoffrey Hinton and Terrence Sejnowski in "To know and to re-learning Boltzmann machines" (1986), but some neurons are identified as input neurons, and others stay "hidden" at the conclusion of a total network upgrade. It ends with arbitrary weights and teaches from the bottom. The neurons primarily have differential activation patterns similar to a Hopfield Net.

The objective of learning for a Boltzmann machine learning algorithm is to maximize the probability of the binary vectors that the machine assigns to the training sets. This is equivalent to minimizing the sum of the log probabilities given to the vectors by the Boltzmann unit. It is also equivalent to maximizing the likelihood that we will get precisely the N training cases if we do: 1) let your network adjust different times to its fixed N distribution, without external input, and 2) sample the visible vector once each time.

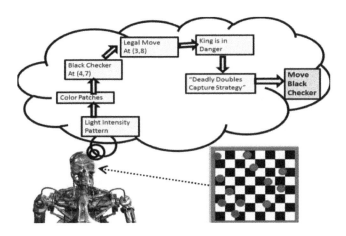

In 2012, an efficient mini-batch learning procedure was proposed by Salakhutdinov and Hinton for Boltzmann Machines.

In the optimistic step, initialize the hidden probabilities at 0.5, clamp a data vector on the observable units and then change all the hidden Units in conjunction with the average field changes to convergence once the net converges, record PiPj for each linked unit pair and mean this in the mini-batch over all the results.

For the negative phase: first, preserve a collection of "fantasy particles," each of which has a global configuration meaning. Review all the units sequentially in each fantasy particle many times. For each pair of associated components, SiSj combines all fantasy particles.

On a Boltzmann system in general, stochastic unit changes must be sequential. There is a specific design for simultaneous, much more effective concurrent changes (no line links, no skip-layer connections). This mini-batch process resembles improvements on the Boltzmann computer. The designation is a Deep Boltzmann Machine (DBM), a Boltzmann general machine with many missed links.

8–Deep Belief Networks

Backpropagation in artificial neural networks is known as the normal way to calculate the error contribution of each neuron after processing the batch of results. Nonetheless, back-propagation causes several major problems. Secondly, labeled training data are required when virtually all data are unlabeled. Secondly, the learning time is not good, which is very slow in multiple hidden layer networks. Second, it can be caught in poor local optima so that they are far from suitable for deep networks.

Researchers have proposed utilizing unregulated learning methods to address the drawbacks of backpropagation. It helps maintain the efficiency and flexibility of using a gradient system for weight change, while also modeling the sensory feedback framework. We specifically change weights to optimize the probability that the sensory input would be produced by a generative model. Which sort of generative model will we learn? Is it like a Boltzmann computer, an energy-based model? Or an idealized neuron causal model? Or the two's hybrid?

Convolutional deep belief networks illustration

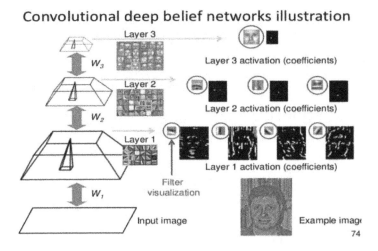

Yoshua Bengio developed Deep Belief Networks ("Greedy deep network layer training"), which were essentially stacked by stack trainable. This strategy is also known as greedy action, which implies greedy options for a reasonable but certainly not ideal answer locally. A confidence net is a directed acyclic graph composed of stochastic variables. We track these variables using the belief system, and we want to address the two problems: 1) the deference problem: the condition of the unknown variables and 2) the question of learning: the modification of the relations between the variables, to make it more feasible for the network to produce results.

Contrasting divergence or retro propagation may educate deep belief networks and learn to interpret data as a probabilistic model. The model can be used for generating new data once it has been learned or converged by unregulated learning to a stable state. Once equipped with opposite divergences, current data can even be identified because the neurons are programmed to look at different characteristics.

9-Autoencoders

Autoencoder is a neural network designed for unattended learning, i.e., unlabelled data. We can be used as data compression templates to transform a specified input into a smaller representation. A decoder can then be used to retrieve the binary representation of the input back.

The research they do is very close to the key part study, which is commonly used to depict a specified object with less than the original number of dimensions. For example, in NLP, you could use PCA to describe a word in 10 numbers if you consider a word as a vector of 100 numbers. Of example, that would contribute to knowledge loss, but it is a safe way to display the data only if you can just function with a small number of dimensions. It is also a good way to visualize details since, in comparison with a 100-dimensional matrix, you can easily track reduced measurements on a 2D graph. The difference is that auto-encoders can use nonlinear transformations to encode the vector into smaller dimensions (compared to the linear PCA) and thus generate more complex encodings.

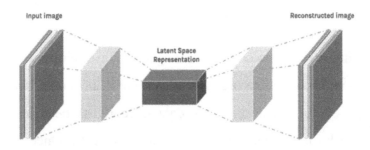

They can be used to minimize dimensions, pretrain other neural networks, generate data, etc. There are several reasons: (1) robust mapping, (2) linear (or better) time in the number of training cases, and (3) fairly compact and fast final coding model. Nevertheless, it turns out that the optimization of deep auto-encoders with backpropagation is very difficult. The back-propagated gradient dies with small initial weights. These are now seldom used in practical applications, primarily because of vanilla-controlled learning best functions in the key areas where it was once deemed breakthroughs (such as layer-wise training). Check Bourlard and Kamp's original 1988 paper.

10 - Generative Adversarial Network

Ian Goodfellow introduced a new breed of neural networks in' Generative Adversarial Nets' (2014) in which two networks collaborate. Generative Adversarial Networks (GANs) consists of two networks, one with a duty to create content (generative), the other with a mission to evaluate information (discriminatory). The discriminatory model has the task of determining whether an image looks natural or artificially created (an image from the dataset). The role of the generator is to create natural representations close to the original data distribution. This can be called a zero-sum or minimal game for two teams. The analogy used in this article is that the generative model is like "a team of counterfeiters, which try to produce and use counterfeit currencies," while the discriminative model is like,' the police, who try to identify the counterfeit currency.' When models are trained through alternating optimization, both methods are enhanced to the extent that "counterfeits are inseparable from the genuine one."

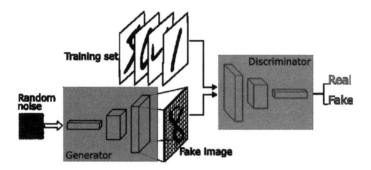

According to Yann LeCun, the next major development could be those networks. These are one of the few effective methods for unsupervised machine learning and revolutionize our capacity to do generative tasks rapidly. We have seen some very impressive results over the last couple of years. There is a great deal of ongoing research in the field to adapt the GANs to language activities, enhance consistency and teaching, etc. These are used in the field for a number of applications, including digital image editing, 3D structure prediction, medicine exploration, and semi-supervised learning, and the robotics sector.

Check this link for a visual and immersive neural network guide

(http://jalammar.github.io/visual-interactive-guide-basics-neural-networks/)

Neural Networks & Artificial Intelligence

Neural networks are known to be "brute force" AI in some circles because they begin with a blank slate and go into a specific model. We are efficient but unsuccessful for some eyes in their computational method, which can not presume practical dependency between output and input.

That said, the descending gradient is not recombining any weight to match the best–the monitoring system decreases the corresponding weight room, and hence the number of changes and measurements available by many order of magnitude. However, algorithms like the capsule networks of Hinton need much fewer data instances to agree on an accurate model. In other terms, existing studies will overcome the brute force complexity of profound thinking.

Neural networks are one of the most innovative paradigms in programming ever conceived. In the conventional programming approach, we tell the computer what to do and break up big problems into many small precise tasks that the computer can perform easily. We do not say the machine, though, how to solve our neural network issues. Instead, it learns from empirical knowledge and seeks its own solution to the problem.

Currently, artificial neural networks and deep learning do well for many important computer vision, speech recognition, and natural language processing problems. They are widely deployed by companies like Google, Microsoft, and Facebook. I hope that this segment can help you learn the basic principles of neural networks and advanced deep learning techniques.

AUTO-ENCODERS

An autoencoder neural network is a back-propagation unattended machine learning algorithm setting the goal values identical to the inputs. Autoencoders are used to reduce the input size to a smaller display. If anybody needs the original data, the compressed data can reconstruct it.

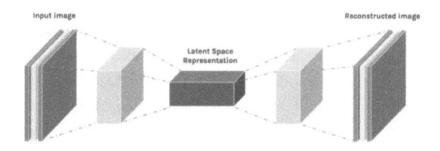

We have a similar algorithm for machine learning. PCA that performs the same task. So why do we need Autoencoders then, could you think? Let's start this Autoencoders Tutorial and understand why Autoencoders are used.

Autoencoders: Its Emergence

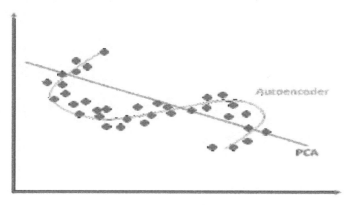

Auto-encoders are preferred to PCAs because:

An auto-encoder teaches non-linear transformations with a non-linear encoding feature and several layers.

It has no thick structures to understand. You can use convolutional layers to know the best for picture, image, and data set.

It is more effective to practice more than one huge transformation with a PCA using an autoencoder.

An autoencoder shows each layer as the performance.

It may use pre-trained layers from another platform to learn how to move to enhance the encoder / decoder.

Now let's look at a range of autoencoder industrial applications.

Autoencoders Applications

Image Coloring

Autoencoders are used to transform any color image into a black and white version. Based on what is on the frame, the color can be decided.

Feature Variation

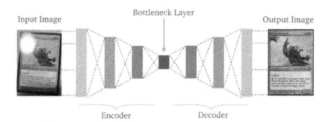

It only extracts the necessary characteristics of an image and produces the output by suppressing any vibration or noise.

Dimensionality Reduction

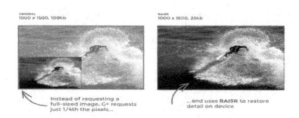

The image reconstructed is the same as our input but with small dimensions. It helps to provide a reduced pixel value for a similar image.

Denoising Image

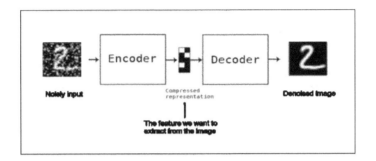

The auto-encoders data is not the original content, but a stochastically distorted form. Thus a denoising self-encoder is learned to recreate the original input from the bright edition.

Watermark Removal

It is also used to erase watermarks or to delete some items when filming a video or film.

Now that you have an overview of the various industrial implementations of autoencoders, let's start with the dynamic architecture of autoencoders.

Architecture Of Autoencoders

The autoencoder is made up of three layers:

- ✓ Encoder
- ✓ Code
- ✓ Decoder

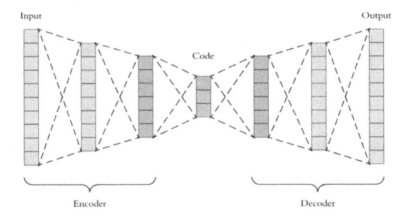

Encoder: This part of the network compresses the data into a latent view. The input picture is represented as a compact file in a reduced dimension. The compressed picture is the blurred image variant.

Code: The compressed input to the decoder is represented in this part of the network.

Decoder: The embedded picture is decoded by this layer into the initial plane. The decoded picture is a lossy reconstruction of a latent version of the original image.

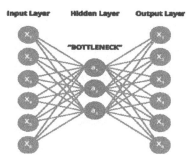

The encoder and decoder layer, i.e., Software, is also referred to as Bottleneck. This is a well-designed method to assess which facets of the findings knowledge are important and which aspects can be ignored. This is achieved by combining two criteria: representation compactness, calculated as compressibility.

It retains certain behaviorally relevant input variables.

Now you have an understanding of an autoencoder's design. Start our Autoencoder Tutorial and grasp the different characteristics and hyperparameters during the training of autoencoders.

Hyperparameters of Autoencoders:

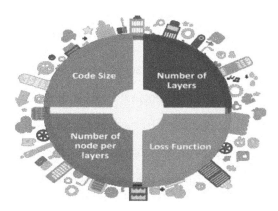

There are 4 hyperparameters that we need to build an autoencoder before training: code size: it shows the number of nodes in the middle layer. More compression results from smaller sizes.

Amount of layers: The autoencoder can be as many layers as we would like.

Amount of nodes per capita: With each following encoder sheet, the amount of nodes per capita reduces and rises back into the decoder. The decoder is symmetrical with the layer configuration of the encoder.

Loss function: we use either squared error or cross-entropy binary. If the input values are in the[0, 1] range, otherwise, cross-entropy is normal, or the mean squared error is used.

Now that you know the features and hyper-parameters of autoencoders school. Let's move on with our Autoencoder Tutorial and get to know the various types of autoencoders and how they differ.

Types of Autoencoders

Convolution Autoencoders

Autoencoders do not believe that a signal can be seen as the sum of other signals in their conventional formulation. Convolutional autoencoders use this statement from the convolution generator. They begin to encrypt the data with basic signals, and then attempt to recreate the picture, alter the structure or the image reflectance.

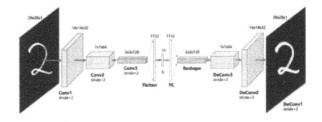

Use cases of CAE:

Image Reconstruction

Image Colorization

latent space clustering

producing advanced resolution images

Sparse Autoencoders

Sparse autoencoders give us an alternate way to introduce a bottleneck knowledge without reducing the number of Nodes in our secret layers. Then, we must build up our loss function to penalize layer activations.

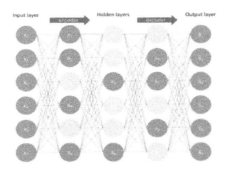

Deep Autoencoders

The Deep Autoencoder is the branch of the simple Autoencoder. Deep Autoencoder's first layer is used for first-order functionality in the raw data. The second layer is used for functions in the second-order, which fit patterns with the presence of features in the first order. Deeper Advanced Autoencoder layers tend to learn much better features.

A deep autoencoder is created by two symmetrical deep-belief networks–first 4 or 5 shallow layers, which constitute the encoding half of the system.

The second set comprises of four or five encoding layers.

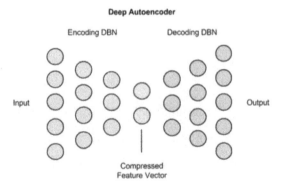

Use cases of Deep Autoencoders:

Image Search

Data Compression

Information Retrieval (IR) & Topic Modeling

Contractive Autoencoders

A contractive self encoder is a non-supervised deep learning strategy that encodes unlabeled training data in a neural network. This can be achieved by building a loss term that penalizes large derivatives of our hidden layer activation regarding the examples of input training, essentially penalizing cases where a small change in the input leads to a big change in the coding area.

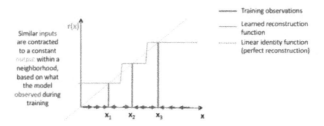

Now that you have an idea of what Autoencoders are, they are different types, and they have different properties. Let's push on by creating the shortest autoencoder possible.

We start simply, with an encoder and a decoder with a single fully connected neural layer:

from keras.layers import Input, Dense

from keras.models import Model

```python
# this is the size of our encoded representations

encoding_dim = 32  # 32 floats -> compression of factor 24.5, assuming the input is 784 floats

# this is our input placeholder

input_img = Input(shape=(784,))

# "encoded" is the encoded representation of the input

encoded = Dense(encoding_dim, activation='relu')(input_img)

# "decoded" is the lossy reconstruction of the input

decoded = Dense(784, activation='sigmoid')(encoded)

# this model maps an input to its reconstruction

autoencoder = Model(input_img, decoded)
```

Let's also create a separate encoder model:

```python
# this model maps an input to its encoded representation

encoder = Model(input_img, encoded)
```

As well as the decoder model:

create a placeholder for an encoded (32-dimensional) input

encoded_input = Input(shape=(encoding_dim,))

retrieve the last layer of the autoencoder model

decoder_layer = autoencoder.layers[-1]

create the decoder model

decoder = Model(encoded_input, decoder_layer(encoded_input))

Now let's train our autoencoder to reconstruct MNIST digits.

First, we'll configure our model to use a per-pixel binary crossentropy loss, and the Adadelta optimizer:

autoencoder.compile(optimizer='adadelta', loss='binary_crossentropy')

Let's prepare our input data. We're using MNIST digits, and we're discarding the labels (since we're only interested in encoding/decoding the input images).

```
from keras.datasets import mnist

import numpy as np

(x_train, _), (x_test, _) = mnist.load_data()
```

We will normalize all values between 0 and 1, and we will flatten the 28x28 images into vectors of size 784.

```
x_train = x_train.astype('float32') / 255.

x_test = x_test.astype('float32') / 255.

x_train = x_train.reshape((len(x_train), np.prod(x_train.shape[1:])))

x_test = x_test.reshape((len(x_test), np.prod(x_test.shape[1:])))

print x_train.shape

print x_test.shape
```

Now let's train our autoencoder for 50 epochs:

```
autoencoder.fit(x_train, x_train,

        epochs=50,

        batch_size=256,

        shuffle=True,

        validation_data=(x_test, x_test))
```

After 50 epochs, the car encoder tends to achieve a constant error value of roughly 0.11. We can try to visualize the inputs reconstructed and the images encoded. We're going to use Matplotlib.

```
# encode and decode some digits

# note that we take them from the *test* set

encoded_imgs = encoder.predict(x_test)

decoded_imgs = decoder.predict(encoded_imgs)

# use Matplotlib (don't ask)

import matplotlib.pyplot as plt
```

```
n = 10  # how many digits we will display

plt.figure(figsize=(20, 4))

for i in range(n):

    # display original

    ax = plt.subplot(2, n, i + 1)

    plt.imshow(x_test[i].reshape(28, 28))

    plt.gray()

    ax.get_xaxis().set_visible(False)

    ax.get_yaxis().set_visible(False)


    # display reconstruction

    ax = plt.subplot(2, n, i + 1 + n)

    plt.imshow(decoded_imgs[i].reshape(28, 28))

    plt.gray()

    ax.get_xaxis().set_visible(False)

    ax.get_yaxis().set_visible(False)

plt.show()
```

This is what we get. Here's what we get. The top row is the original numbers, and the bottom row is the reconstructed numbers. With this basic approach, we are missing quite a bit of detail.

Note: that's is just a basic approach. You can learn the more advanced input fro below link

https://blog.keras.io/building-autoencoders-in-keras.html

EM ALGORITHM AND APPLICATIONS

Total likelihood calculation is a density approximation method for a sample by looking for probability distribution and its parameters.

It is a common and effective approach that underlies several machine-learning algorithms, although the testing dataset has to be full, for example, all applicable variables that communicate spontaneously are present. Maximum probability is unlikely if variables interact with those in the dataset but hide or fail to observe so-called latent variables.

The expectation-maximization algorithm is a method to approximate maximum likelihood when latent variables are present. Next, the value for the latent variables is calculated, then the process modified, then the two measures are replicated before convergence is reached. It is a common, efficient way of estimating the density with a lack of data, such as grouping algorithms, such as the Gaussian Mixture Model.

Latent Variables Problem

A common modeling problem involves estimating a joint likelihood distribution for a dataset.

The density estimation includes a distributed function of likelihood and the parameters of that distribution, which best explains the combined distribution of the probability of the results observed.

There are many approaches to solve this problem, although a common approach is called the maximum probability calculation or simply the maximum probability. A maximum probability estimate includes treating the problem as an optimization or search problem while finding a collection of parameters to best suit the joint likelihood of the data sample.

A maximal chance evaluation constraint is that the sample is believed to be total or completely tested. This does not imply that the model has access to all details, but that all variables related to the question are available.

It's not always the case. Datasets can only be identified with a few of the relevant variables, and some cannot be detected, and although they affect certain random variables in the dataset, they are still concealed.

Most commonly, these unknown or hidden variables are considered latent variables.

Most real-world issues include implicit variables (sometimes named latent ones), which can not be detected in the data available for study.

Conventional high likelihood calculations in the case of latent variables do not function well.

If we have incomplete details and/or latent variables, it's difficult to calculate the[maximum probability] calculation.

Alternatively, the hunt for the necessary model parameters in the presence of latent variables involves an alternative approximation of the highest probability.

Another such strategy is the Expectation-Maximization algorithm.

ML | Expectation-Maximization Algorithm

For real-world machine learning implementations, it is very typical that there are plenty of specific learning functions usable, but only a small subset can be seen. Therefore, for variables that are sometimes observable or not, we can use the occasions when the variable is apparent to the learning intention and then estimate its meaning when not detected.

On the other hand, the latent variables (variables not directly observed and derived from the values of the other measured variables) can be used to estimate their values, with the assumption that the general form of probability distribution controlling such latent variables is well understood to us. In addition, this algorithm is the foundation for many unattended clustering algorithms in machine learning.

In a paper published in 1977 by Arthur Dempster, Nan Laird, and Donald Rubin, it was described, suggested, and named. The local maximum probability parameters of a statistical model are found where there are latent variables and the data is missing or incomplete.

Algorithm:

Consider a collection of starting parameters in view of a set of incomplete data.

Expectation step (E-step): estimate (assume) the values of the missing data, using observed available dataset data.

The phase of maximization (M–phase): full data generated following stage of expectation (E) is used to update the parameters.

Repeat steps 2 and 3 until convergence.

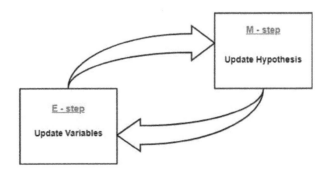

It is important to use the available data from the dataset to approximate the missing data and then use the data to correct the parameter values. Let us explain in depth the EM algorithm.

Specific consideration is given to a set of specific parameter values. The framework provides a series of partially observed data on the basis that the observed data come from a particular model.

The next step is called "Expectation"–phase or E-step. In this stage, we use the data we analyze to approximate or estimate the values of the missing or incomplete data. It is used to change the variables.

The next step is called "Maximization" or M-Step. In this stage, we use the complete information produced in the previous "Expectation" step to update the parameter values. It is used primarily for testing the theory.

The fourth step will now evaluate whether the values agree or not, if so, otherwise stop repeating step 2 and step 3 otherwise, i.e.' Expectation'–step and' Maximisation' –step up to convergence.

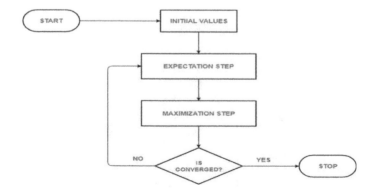

Usage of EM algorithm –

It can be utilized to fill the missing information in a sample.

It can be utilized as the basis of not being watched learning of clusters.

It can be used for the purpose of approximating the parameters of the Hidden Markov Model (HMM).

It can be used to discover the values of hidden variables.

Benefits of EM algorithm--.

It is constantly guaranteed that the possibility will increase with each model.

The E-step and M-step are typically pretty simple for numerous issues in terms of application.

Solutions to the M-steps often exist in the closed-form.

Drawbacks of EM algorithm--.

It has slow merging.

It makes convergence to the local optima just.

It needs both the probabilities, forward and backward (mathematical optimization requires only forward probability).

Build Better And Accurate Clusters With Gaussian Mixture Models

I like to focus on unattended learning problems. We pose a totally different task for a guided learning problem–there is much more space to play with the data I have. No wonder the bulk of inventions and advancements in the machine learning domain arise in the unmonitored field of research.

And clustering is one of the most common strategies in unattended research. Normally, this is a term we learn early on in our machine learning path, and it's easy enough to understand. I'm sure that you met or worked on projects such as customer segmentation, market basket analysis, etc.

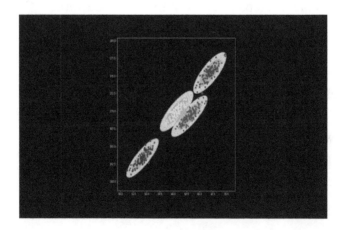

But this is the thing–clustering has a lot of layers. It is not limited to the fundamental algorithms that we have learned before. It is an efficient, unattended learning methodology that we can use with unfailing precision in the real world.

Gaussian Mixture Models are one algorithm I want to speak about in this portion.

Would you like to predict your favorite product sales? Or you might want to understand customer churning through various customer groups. Regardless of the use case, Gaussian Mixture Models are really useful.

In this section, we will take a bottom-top approach. So first, we look at the fundamentals of clustering, with a quick overview of the k-means algorithm. Then we'll dive into and implement the concept of Gaussian models in Python.

Introduction To Clustering

Let's refresh some basic concepts quickly before we start things and enter the nitty rhythm of the Gaussian Mixture Models.

Note: When you know the principle behind clustering and the way the k-media algorithm operates, you should skip straight to the fourth part, "Gaussian Mixture Models Introduction." Note:

Let us, therefore, begin by defining the core idea formally: the clustering refers to the collection of like data points based on their attributes or features.

For starters, if we have the income and expenses for a certain number of people, we will divide them into the following groups:

- ✓ Earn high, spend high
- ✓ Earn high, spend low
- ✓ Earn low, spend low
- ✓ Earn low, spend high

Each of these categories would have similar characteristics and could help to pitch the specific scheme / product into the community. Talk about credit cards, car loans, etc. To put it simply: the concept behind clustering is to pool together data points so that each cluster has the most similar points.

Different clustering algorithms are usable. K-means is one of the most common clustering algorithms. Let's understand how the algorithm K-means works and the scenarios where this algorithm is not expected.

Introduction to k-means Clustering

k-means clustering is an algorithm based on distance. It tries to group the closest points in order to form a cluster.

Let's look at the working of this algorithm. This will lay the groundwork for understanding where Gaussian Mixture Models will be played later in this segment.

We first define the number of groups in which the population is to be divided, which is k. We then randomly initialize K centroids based on the number of clusters or groups we like.

The data points are then allocated to the nearest center, and a cluster is formed. The centers will be updated, and the data points reassigned. The process continues until the position of the centers no longer varies.

Drawbacks Of K-Means Clustering

The clustering concept sounds pretty good, right? It is easy to understand, easy to deploy, and can be applied in a number of applications. But we need to be mindful of certain risks and limits.

Using the same illustration of profit spending we discussed above. The k-means algorithm looks pretty good, right? Hold on–you will notice that all of the created clusters have a circular shape if you look closely. This is because the centers of the clusters are modified with the mean value.

Consider the case below, where the distribution of points is not spherical. What do you think will happen if we use k-means on these data? It would still try to group the data points circularly. That's not great! That's not great! k-means does not understand the correct clusters:

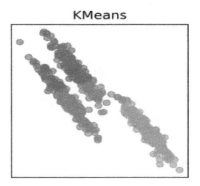

We, therefore, need another way of assigning clusters to data points. We are now using a distribution-based model rather than using a distance-based model. So Gaussian Mixture Models come in this section!

A Gaussian Mixture Models (GMMs) implementation Gaussian Mixture Models (GMMs) presume that a certain number of Gaussian distributions exist, and each of these distributions is a cluster. A

Gaussian Mixture Model tends to group together the data points of a single distribution.

Let's just say we have three Gaussian distributions–GD1, GD2, and GD3 (more on this next section). These have a mean value ($\mu1$, $\mu2$, $\mu3$) and a variance value($\beta1$, $\beta2$, $\mu3$) respectively. Our GMM would identify the probability of each data point in each of the distributions for a given number of data points.

Stop, Yes, Way?

You read, right! Gaussian Mixture models are probabilistic and use a soft clustering approach in order to spread the points through different clusters. I'm going to take another example to make things easier to understand.

There are three clusters here, named Blue, Green, and Cyan, which are three colors. Let's take the red colored data point. The probability that this point is in the blue cluster is 1, but that it is in the green or cyan cluster is 0.

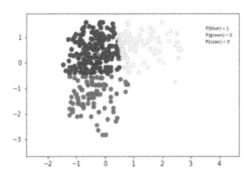

Take another argument–between the blue and cyan somewhere (emphasized in the figure below). The probability that this is a component of cluster green is 0, right? And the probability is 0.2 and 0.8 respectively for blue and cyan.

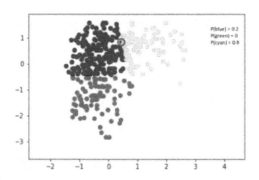

The soft clustering technique is used by Gaussian Mixture Models to assign data points in Gaussian distributions. I'm sure you wonder what those distributions are, so let me clarify this in the following section.

I am sure you know the Gaussian Distribution (or the Normal Distribution). The Gaussian Distribution. It has a clock-shaped pattern, with the data points spread symmetrically around the baseline.

The picture below displays many Gaussian distributions with a mean (μ) and variance ($\mu2$). Remember that the higher the μ value, the greater the spread:

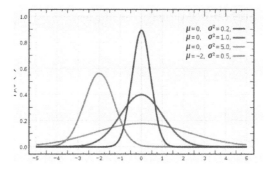

Source: Wikipedia

The probability density function of a Gaussian distribution is given in a single dimension space:

$$f(x \mid \mu, \sigma^2) = \frac{1}{\sqrt{2\pi\sigma^2}} e^{-\frac{(x-\mu)^2}{2\sigma^2}}$$

where the standard is μ, and the deviation is 2.

Nonetheless, this would only refer to a single variable. For 2 variables, we have a 3D bell curve instead of a 2D bell curve, as shown below:

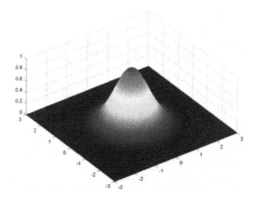

The function of probability density would be:

$$f(x \mid \mu, \Sigma) = \frac{1}{\sqrt{2\pi|\Sigma|}} \exp\left[-\tfrac{1}{2}(x-\mu)'\Sigma^{-1}(x-\mu)\right]$$

Where x is the reference vector, μ is the standard 2D vector, and μ is the covariance function of 2 numbers. The covariance would now determine the curve's form. For d-dimensions, we can generalize the same.

This Gaussian multivariate construct would, therefore, have x and μ as length vectors d and os would be dx d covariance matrix.

Therefore we would have a combination of k Gaussian distributions for a dataset with d characteristics (where k corresponds to the number of clusters), each with a medium vector and variance matrix. But wait– how is each Gaussian assigned mean and variance value?

These values are determined using the Expect-Maximization (EM) technique. Before we go into the work of Gaussian Mixture Models, we have to understand this technique.

Expectation-Maximization In Gaussian Mixture Models

Let's take another example to see this. I want you to imagine the image when you hear it. This will help you understand better what we are talking about.

Let's say we have k number of clusters to assign. In other terms, k Gaussian distributions with a mean covariance value of $\mu 1$, $\mu 2$,.. μk and $\mu k\ 1$, μk and μk, μk and μk Towards the end of the day, In fact, there is another distribution function that determines the distribution number of points. Or in other words, the distribution density is represented by, ie.

Now we must find the values for the Gaussian distributions for these parameters. We've already determined the number of clusters and assigned the mean, covariance, and density values arbitrarily. We'll do the E-step and the M-step next!

E-step:

Calculate the probability of cluster / distribution c1, c2,... ck for each dot xi. This is achieved with the following formula:

$$r_{ic} = \frac{\text{Probability Xi belongs to c}}{\text{Sum of probability Xi belongs to } c_1, c_2, .. c_k} = \frac{\pi_c \mathcal{N}(x_i \ ; \ \mu_c, \Sigma_c)}{\sum_{c'} \pi_{c'} \mathcal{N}(x_i \ ; \ \mu_{c'}, \Sigma_{c'})}$$

This importance is strong when the point is applied to the correct cluster and lower.

M-step: post-e-step, go back to change the meaning of índice, μ, and da. The following was updated: the current density is defined by the ratio of points in the cluster and the total number of points:

$$\Pi = \frac{\text{Number of points assigned to cluster}}{\text{Total number of points}}$$

The mean and covariance matrix was modified in relation to the likelihood values for the point based on the values applied to the distribution. Thus, a data point which is more likely to be part of this distribution contributes a greater part:

$$\mu = \frac{1}{\text{Number of points assigned to cluster}} \Sigma_i \, r_{ic} x_i$$

$$\Sigma_c = \frac{1}{\text{Number of points assigned to cluster}} \Sigma_i \, r_{ic} \, (x_i - \mu_c)^T (x_i - \mu_c)$$

Based on the updated data from this step, the new probabilities for each data point are calculated, and the values updated iteratively. This process is repeated to maximize the log-like feature. We might effectively say that k-means just find the way to change the centroid when GMM takes the mean and variation of the results into account!

In Python, it is time to dive in the code! Implementing Gaussian Mixture Models We're going to start loading the files.

```
import pandas as pd


data = pd.read_csv('Clustering_gmm.csv')
```

```
plt.figure(figsize=(7,7))

plt.scatter(data["Weight"],data["Height"])

plt.xlabel('Weight')

plt.ylabel('Height')

plt.title('Data Distribution')

plt.show()
```

view rawdata_distribution.py hosted with   by GitHub

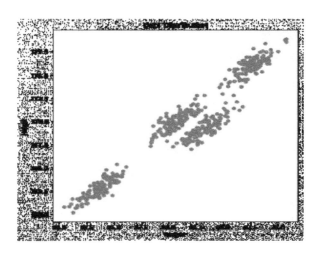

This is how our data looks. Let's first create a k-means model on this data:

```
#training k-means model

from sklearn.cluster import KMeans

kmeans = KMeans(n_clusters=4)

kmeans.fit(data)

#predictions from kmeans

pred = kmeans.predict(data)

frame = pd.DataFrame(data)

frame['cluster'] = pred

frame.columns = ['Weight', 'Height', 'cluster']

#plotting results

color=['blue','green','cyan', 'black']

for k in range(0,4):
```

```
data = frame[frame["cluster"]==k]

plt.scatter(data["Weight"],data["Height"],c=color[k])

plt.show()
```

view rawbuilding_kmeans.py hosted with   by GitHub

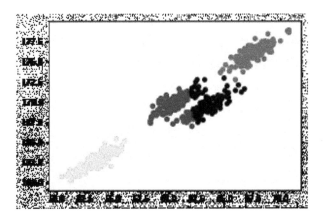

That is not quite right. This is not quite right. The variable k-means could not classify the right clusters. Look closely at the clusters in the center–k-means has tried to build a circular cluster, even if the distribution of data is elliptical.

Let us now construct a Gaussian Mixture Model using the same details and see whether k-means can be improved:

```
import pandas as pd
```

```
data = pd.read_csv('Clustering_gmm.csv')

# training gaussian mixture model

from sklearn.mixture import GaussianMixture

gmm = GaussianMixture(n_components=4)

gmm.fit(data)

#predictions from gmm

labels = gmm.predict(data)

frame = pd.DataFrame(data)

frame['cluster'] = labels

frame.columns = ['Weight', 'Height', 'cluster']

color=['blue','green','cyan', 'black']

for k in range(0,4):

    data = frame[frame["cluster"]==k]

    plt.scatter(data["Weight"],data["Height"],c=color[k])

plt.show()
```

view rawgaussian_mixture_model.py hosted with   by GitHub

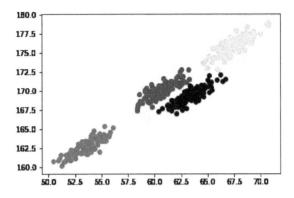

Excellent! Excellent! These are the clusters we all wished for. The Gaussian Mixture Models have blown k-means here from the water.

Endnotes

This was a Gaussian Mixture guide for beginners. My purpose here was to expose you to this effective clustering technology and illustrate the reliability and performance of your algorithms.

I invite you to conduct a clustering project and check GMMs. This is the best way to learn and implement a method–so trust me to know how important it algorithm is.

LINEAR REGRESSION FOR MACHINE LEARNING

Linear regression is perhaps one of the most well-known and understood statistical and machine learning algorithms.

You can explore in this segment the linear regression method, how it operates, and how best to use it in the machine learning ventures. In this segment, you can learn: why both statistics and machine learning have linear regression.

The many terms that are recognized for linear regression.

The methods used to describe and learn used to construct a linear regression model.

How to best prepare the data for linear regression analysis.

To grasp linear regression, you do not need to learn any mathematics or linear algebra. This is a gentle high-level introduction to the technology to help you to use it effectively on your own problems.

Let's start. Let's get started.

Isn't Simple Statistical Regression?

You might be wondering why we are looking at this algorithm before we dive into the details of linear regression.

Isn't this a mathematical technique?

The main aim of Machine Learning is to reduce the error of a prediction or to render the most precise predictions possible, at the cost of explainability. We borrow, reuse, and steal algorithms in applied machine learning from many different fields, including statistics, and use them for that purpose.

In the world of statistics, linear regression was developed as a paradigm to comprehend the associations between numerical variables of input and output but was borrowed from machine learning. It is both a mathematical algorithm and an application for smart computers.

Then let's take a look at some of the common names for the linear regression model.

Many Names Of Linear Regression

Once you begin to look at linear regression, it can become very complicated.

The reason is that there has been a linear regression over so long (over 200 years). Each angle has been researched, and often each angle has a new and different tag.

Linear regression is a linear model; for instance, a model that assumes that the input variables (x) are linearly linked to the single output variable (y). In particular, you can calculate from a linear combination of the input variables(x).

When the input variable (x) exists, the method is known as a simple linear regression. If several input variables exist, mathematical literature also refers to the approach as multiple linear regression.

The most widely recognized is the ordinary least squares; the linear regression algorithm can be primed or educated using different techniques. Therefore, a model prepared in this way is commonly referred to as the ordinary lower places linear regression or just the lower placed regression.

Now that we know certain names used for linear regression, please discuss the description used more closely.

Linear Regression Model Representation

Linear regression is an appealing paradigm because it is so easy to depict.

This is a linear equation that combines a specific set of input values (x), and the solution for that set of input values is the predicted output (y). The input (x) values, as well as the output value, are numerical.

-input value or column referred to as a coefficient and described with the capital Greek letter Beta (B), is allocated one scale factor. There is also an additional coefficient, which gives the line additional freedom (e.g., up-and downward movement) and is often referred to as an intercept or bisection coefficient.

For example, the form of the model in a simple (a single x and a single y) regression problem would be: $y = B0 + B1*x$ If we have more than one input (x), the line is called a plane or a superficial plane. Therefore, the representation is the shape of the equation and the different values used for coefficients (e.g., B0 and B1 in the case above).

The sophistication of a regression model, such as linear regression, is normal. The number of coefficients used in the model refers to this.

When a coefficient is zero, then the effect of the input variable on the model and thus the prediction from the model ($0*x = 0$) is effectively eliminated. This becomes important when you see regularization techniques, which adjust the learning process, by manipulating the absolute size of coefficients to decrease the difficulty of regression models, reducing some to zero.

Now that we understand how a linear regression model is represented, let us look at some of the ways we can learn this from data.

Linear Regression - Learning The Model

To learn a linear regression model means to estimate the values of the representation coefficients with the data we possess.

In this portion, we will discuss four strategies for the preparation of a linear regression model. This is not enough knowledge to execute it from start to finish, but enough to get a feel for programming and rewards.

Many more methods are accessible because the pattern is learned so well. Please note that the Ordinary Least Squares are the most common method used commonly. Take note of Gradient Descent as it is the most common method of machine learning.

1. Simple linear regression

If there is a single sample, we can use statistics to approximate the parameters using simple linear regression.

It includes the estimation of statistical data properties such as processes, standard deviations, associations, and covariance. Everything evidence must be accessible for information to be traversed and measured.

This is enjoyable as an excellent workout, but not really effective in practice.

2. Ordinary Last Squares

We can use ordinary Last Squares to approximate the coefficient values by using more than one parameter.

Ordinary Least Squares aims to reduce the sum of squared residues to a minimum. It implies that in the case of a regression line via the results, we measure the duration from each data point to the regression line, square it, and sum together all the squared errors. This is the sum that regular squares want to reduce.

This approach treats data as a matrix and uses linear algebra operations to determine the optimum coefficient values. This means all data must be available, and sufficient memory must be available to fit the data and perform matrix operations.

It is rare to execute the Ordinary Least Squares method yourself except as a linear algebra exercise. You are more likely to call a method in a linear library of algebra. This procedure can be calculated very quickly.

3. Gradient descent

If one or more inputs exist, you can use a process to optimize the coefficients ' values by reducing the model error on your training data iteratively.

This operation is referred to as Gradient descent and starts with random values for each coefficient. For each pair of input and output values, the sum of the squared errors is calculated. A learning rate is used as a scaling factor, and the parameters are modified to minimize the error. The process is repeated until a minimum amount of error has been met, or there is no more progress.

You have to select the learning rate (alpha) parameter when using this method to determine the size of the improvement step to be taken in each procedure isolation.

Gradient descent is often taught using a linear regression model because it is quite easy to understand. For reality, when you have a very large data collection, it is useful just to include the number of rows or columns that can not fit in the brain.

4. Regularization

The training of the linear model known as regularization methods has been extended. Such work at decreasing both the amount of the model's squared error in training data (using the ordinary least squares) but also the sophistication of the model (such as its number or absolute size).

The Lasso Regression: where the ordinary least squares are adjusted to minimize the absolute amount of coefficients, is two common examples of regularization procedures for linear regression.

Ridge regression: everywhere, ordinary lower places have been adjusted to minimize the squared absolute sum of the coefficients (called regularization of L2).

Such techniques are useful if your input values are collinear, and the normal smallest positions will surpass the training data.

Now that you have learned some methods in a linear regression model of coefficients, let's look at how we can use a model to predict new data.

Making Predictions with Linear Regression

Given that representation is a linear equation, predictions are so simple that the equation for a specific set of inputs is solved.

Let's give an example to render this concrete. Imagine weight (y) is predicted from height (x). For this question, our linear regression model representation would be:

y = B0 + B1 * x1

or

weight =B0 +B1 * height

Where B0 is the bias coefficient, and B1 is the height column coefficient. We use an apprenticeship to find a good set of values. Once it is found, different height values can be plugged into to predict weight.

Let us use, for example, B0= 0.1 and B1= 0.5. Let's plug it in and measure the weight (in kilograms) for a human 182 cm long.

weight = 0.1 + 0.5 * 182

weight = 91.1

You can see that the equation above can be traced as a two-dimensional line. The B0 is our starting point regardless of our height. We can run from 100 to 250 centimeters through a bunch of heights, and plug it into the equation and obtain weight values.

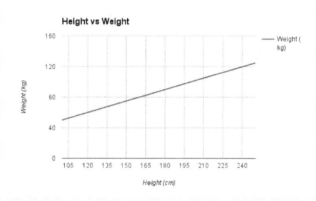

Sample Height vs. Weight Linear Regression

Now that we know how to predict a linear regression model, let's look at some guidelines for preparing our data to take advantage of this type of model.

Preparing Data For Linear Regression

Linear regression is extensively studied, and a great deal of literature is available on how your data should be structured to make the best use of the model.

Furthermore, there is a lot of daunting complexity to think about these criteria and aspirations. For reality, you should allow more use of such principles as thumb rules when using the most popular version of linear regression, Ordinary Least Squares Regression.

Use these heuristics to try out different arrangements of your data and see how the question works best.

Linear Assumption

Normal regression means that your input-output relationship is normal. This helps nothing else. This may be obvious, but remember that you have many attributes. It is good to remember. You might need to transform data in order to make the relationship linear (e.g., for exponential relationship log transformation).

Remove Noise

Linear regression assumes that noise is not present in your input and output variables. Consider using data cleaning operations to make the signal in your data, better known and clarified. This is most important for the output variable, and if necessary, you can exclude outliers in the output variable (y).

Remove Collinearity

Linear regression can overfit the data when the input variables are highly correlated. Try measuring and extracting the most important associations for your data.

Gaussian Distributions.

If your input and output variables have a Gaussian distribution, linear regression will make more reliable predictions. You will benefit from converting the variables (e.g., log or BoxCox) to optimize their distribution to Gaussian.

Rescale Inputs:

Linear regression is often more reliable if you rescale input variables by standardization or standardization.

See this connection for complete implementation of the code

(https://github.com/SSaishruthi/Linear_Regression_Detailed_Implem entation)

LOGISTIC REGRESSION FOR MACHINE LEARNING

The approach taken from deep learning from the world of analytics is logistic regression.

This is the go-to approach for binary classification problems (two-class value problems). In this segment, you can find the machine learning practical regression algorithm.

Logistic Function

For the function used at the core of the process, the logistic function is named logistic regression.

Statisticians developed the logistic function, also known as Sigmoid Function, to describe the properties of population growth in ecology, rising rapidly and increasing environmental capacity. It is an S-formed curve that can take any true numbers and map them into value from 0 to 1, but never at those limits exactly.

1 / (1 + e^-value) Where e is the basis of your table of natural logarithms (Euler's or EXP) (functions) and value is the real numerical value you would like to transform. The following is a list of numbers between-5 and 5 transformed by the logistic function into a range of 0 and 1.

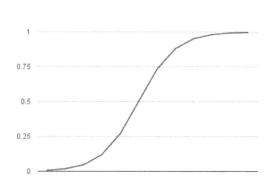

Logistic Function

Now that we know what the logistic function is, let's see what the logistic function is used for.

Representation Used for logistic regression

The regression of logistics is similar to the linear regression using an equation as representation.

Input value(x) are combined linearly to predict output value (Y) by using weights or coefficient values (referred to as the Greek capital letter Beta). A key difference from the linear regression is that the significance of the production is not a numerical number but a binary value (0 or 1).

The following is an example of the equation of logistic regression: $y= \bar{e}(b0+ b1*x) / (1+e^{\wedge}(b0+ b1*x))$ where y is the expected performance, b0 is the terminal of bias or interception, and b1 is the single value coefficient (x). The related b-coefficient (a constant real value) is expected to be obtained from your training data in each column of your input data.

The real expression of the formula in the memory or in a register is the coefficients in the equation (beta value or b's).

Logistic Regression Predicts Probabilities (Technical Interlude)

The likelihood of a default class (e.g., first class) is modeled by logistic regression.

For example, if we model the sex of the people as male or female from their heights, the first-class might be male, and the logistic regression model could be written as the probability of a man's height or more formally: P(sex= male) Written; differently, we model the likelihood that an input(x) would belong to the standard class (Y=1), and that we can write it formally as:

P(X)

I figured logistic regression was an algorithm of classification?

Remember that the chance calculation should be converted into binary values (0 or 1) to estimate the likelihood accurately. More about this later, as we think about forecasting.

Logistic regression is a linear procedure, but the logistic function is used to convert the predictions. The consequences of this are that the projections can not be seen anymore as linear iterations of the inputs, for example, if you continue from above, you may suggest the formula as:

$(p(X) = e^{\wedge}(b0 + b1 * X) / (1 + e^{\wedge}(b0 + b1 * X))$

I don't want to delve into math, but we can go around the equation as follows (note that we may delete the e from one side by ad).

The normal party odds are referred to as this formula on the left (historical, for example, odds are used in horse racing instead of probability). Odds are calculated as a measure of the event likelihood divided by the event chance, e.g., 0.8/(1-0.8), which has an odds of 4.

Alternatively, we might write: $\ln(odds) = b0 + b1 * X$

As the odds are converted, we label log-odds or probit from the left side. Any other kind of function can be used (which is out of scope but is usually referenced in the transformation that relates the linear regression equation to probabilities as a link function, for example, the probit link function.

The exponent is moved back to the right, and it is written as odds (e^(b0 + b1 * X)).

Learning the Logistic Regression Model

Your training data should be used to approximate coefficients (Beta values b) of the logistic regression algorithm. This is done with a maximum estimate of likelihood.

Maximum likelihood estimates are a common learning algorithm used by a variety of machine learning algorithms, but it does make assumptions about the distribution of your data.

The optimal equations will result in a formula that would estimate for the default class a value very near 1 (e.g., male) and for the other class a value very similar to 0 (e.g., female). The maximal logistic regression principle is that a scanning method searches for coefficient values (beta values), which decrease the error of the model-predicted probabilities of those in the data (i.e., the likelihood of 1 if the data is of the primary class).

We won't go into the analysis of the highest chance. Suffice it to say that a minimization algorithm is used to optimize the best values for your training data's coefficients. This is usually done with an effective numerical optimization method (similar to the quasi-newton procedure).

If you are learning logistics, the much simpler gradient descent algorithm can implement it yourself from scratch.

Making Predictions With Logistic Regression

Predictions using a logistic regression model are just as straightforward as plugs in numbers and the estimation of a consequence into the logistic regression equation.

With a specific example, let's make this concrete.

Let's assume we have a model that can determine whether a person is male or female by height (full of fiction). The individual is male or female at the height of 150 cm.

The coefficients of b0= -100 and b1= 0.6 have been learned. The above equation helps us to measure the likelihood of a person at or more formally P(male) provided 150 cm height. We will use EXP) (for e, as you can use it if you type this illustration into your tablet:

$y = e^{(b0 + b1*X)} / (1 + e^{(b0 + b1*X)})$

$y = \exp(-100 + 0.6*150) / (1 + EXP(-100 + 0.6*X))$

$y = 0.0000453978687$

Or a near-zero likelihood that the individual is a man.

For reality, we will simply use the odds. Since that's classification and we want a limited response, for example, we may snap the probabilities into a binary class value:

0 if p(male) < 0.5

1 if p(male) >= 0.5

Now that we can use logistic regression to make predictions let us look at how we can plan our data to get the most out of this methodology.

Prepare Data For Logistic Regression

The logistic regression on distribution and associations in your data is much the same as the linear regression assumptions.

Several experiments have been carried out to establish these hypotheses, and valid probabilistic and predictive systems are used. I recommend using them as guidelines or thumb rules and experimenting with various data preparation programs.

For predictive modeling machine learning programs, you center laser on forecasting correctly rather than interpreting the results. As such, you can break certain assumptions as long as the model is robust and functional.

Binary output variable: This could be obvious, as we mentioned earlier, but logistic regression is for binary (two-class) classification problems. This estimates the chance for an instance of the default class that can be marked as 0 or 1.

Noise removal: Logistic regression does not take into account an error in the output variable (y); it considers removing outliers and eventually misclassified instances from your training data.

Gaussian Distribution: Logistic regression is a linear (nonlinear) algorithm. This implies a continuous relation between the input and output variables. Information transforming the input variables which reveal this linear relationship better will contribute to a more accurate model. To order to understand this relationship better, you can use log, base, Box-Cox, and other univariates, for example.

Disable Associated Inputs: The model is likely to overfit, as with linear regression, if there are several highly correlated inputs. Try estimating differences between all inputs on a pair basis and eliminating highly correlated inputs.

Failure to converge: the predicted probability assessment process will contribute to coefficients failure to converge. This may happen when your data has many highly correlated inputs or if the data (e.g., many zeros in your input data) is very sparse.

ENSEMBLE METHODS IN MACHINE LEARNING: WHAT ARE THEY, AND WHY USE THEM?

If you want to buy a new car, are you going to the first auto shop and buy one on the recommendation of the dealer? It's very doubtful.

You should typically visit a few web portals where you have posted comments and compare different car models to test their specifications and costs. You're probably also going to ask your friends and colleagues to comment. In short, you would not reach a direct conclusion but instead will make a decision taking into account the opinions of other people.

Machine learning models work on a similar idea. We blend the options of several designers to improve overall efficiency.

What are they, Ensemble Methods?

Ensemble methods are a machine learning process that combines a number of basic models to create an optimized predictive model. This concept helps you to step back into the ultimate aim of machine learning and model creation. This is more helpful as I immerse myself in specific examples and why Ensemble approaches are used.

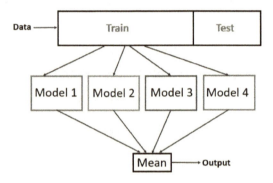

I would primarily use Decision Trees to explain Ensemble Methods ' meanings and practicality (it is, however, important to note that Ensemble Methods do not only refer to Decision Trees).

Based on a number of questions and conditions, a Decision Tree determines the predictive value. A basic decision tree decides, for example, whether a person can play outside or not. The tree takes into account various weather conditions and either make a decision or poses another question in terms of each aspect. In this case, we play outside every time it's rainy. If it rains, however, should we ask whether it's windy or not? If we're windy, we won't play. But because there was no storm, tie those shoelaces tightly because they were playing outdoors.

A Decision Tree

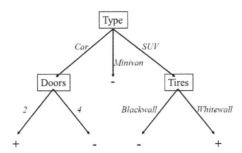

Decision Trees can also address mathematical problems in the same style. We would like to know whether or not to invest in a commercial immobilization in the Tree to the left. Is it a place for an office? Warehouse? A warehouse? A house for an apartment? Good conditions for the economy? Poor economic circumstances? How much is the return on investment going to be? A decision tree addresses and tackles certain concerns.

There are several considerations that we need to take into account when making decisions on trees: what are the characteristics of our decision? What is the threshold for a Yes or No answer in each question? What if we wanted to ask ourselves whether or not we had friends to play with at the first decision tree. If we have friends, every time we play. If not, we could still ask ourselves whether questions. We hope to describe the Yes and No groups further by including a further query.

Ensemble approaches come in handy here! Ensemble approaches allow us to take into account a number of decision trees rather than simply rely on a decision tree and hope we made the right choice in each split, determine the features you should use or inquire in each split and generate a final prediction on the basis of the aggregated effects of the decision trees tested.

Three most common Ensemble methods

Bagging

bagging is a general strategy for integrating the results of a number of models, short for bootstrap aggregation. While it can be used for aggregating the outputs of all regression or classification models, it is usually used in decision-making bodies. The' bootstrap' bagging component only means that you have a set of observations that are randomly sampled by the replacement of your original training data on each individual tree. Nevertheless, you create many of these trees and then combine them. For classification problems, a majority vote of all the trees in your model would generate your aggregated predictions. Your estimate for regression problems would only be an average performance of the trees.

Random Forests

Some of the strongest models today are random forests. The adaptation of your decision trees to the bootstrapped data can be slightly decorated. Since each node selects the function you want to divide in gullible fashion, the trees can still be very correlated. Random forests add another step towards decorating the individual decision-making trees. When the CART algorithm selects for each node the optimal split, the random forest chooses a random subset of your characteristics and only takes account of the ones for that split. The algorithm also chooses the best function from this random subset of features and divides to create each node.

Extremely randomized trees

Extremely randomized trees, abbreviated as ExtraTrees in Sklearn, adds a further randomization step to the random forestry algorithm. Random forests can determine the optimal break in the randomly selected subset for distance, and choose the best feature to separate. ExtraTrees picks a random split for each characteristic in that random subset and then selects the better characteristic to break by matching randomly selected splits. Extremely random trees are much more effective in computing than random forests and almost always have comparable performance. In some instances, they can do even more!

My thoughts

The objective of any problem of machine learning is to find a single model that best predicts our desired outcome. The ensemble approaches take into account a multitude of variables, rather than the highest / most reliable prediction we would create for one model and expect for this one, then combine all models to generate the final result. It is worth noting that Decision Trees are not only the most common and important type of ensemble methods in data science today.

DEEP LEARNING WITH TENSORFLOW: THEORY AND SETUP

Tensorflow is the most common and clearly best in the field of deep learning. Why is it?

TensorFlow is a Google-created platform for creating Deep Learning models. Deep learning is an engine learning model category(= algorithms) using neural multi-layer networks.

Machine Learning enabled us to create complex applications with great precision. Regardless of whether it is about images, videos, text, or even audio, machine learning can solve a wide range of problems. For all such applications, TensorFlow can be used.

The justification for its success is the simple way to build and install applications. We should look closer to the GitHub projects because the following pieces are very strong but easy to work with. In addition, Tensorflow with processing power limitations in mind has been developed. The library can be run on all kinds of computers, even on smartphones (yes, with half an apple on it). I will promise that you will not have any performance problems when running on an Intel Core i3 with 8 GB of RAM.

But we have to understand a basic concept before we know Tensorflow. How can we "talk" our machines?

The human brain is made up of billions of neurons connected by synapses. When synaptic signals are adequate for the neuron flames, the neuron always burns. This method is alluded to as feeling. We need a machine learning and neural networks to reproduce this mechanism on computers. If you don't consent to these words, I'm going to explain them.

Machine learning:

Simply put, machine learning can' learn' computers. Traditionally, computers have always had to do things with a strict set of instructions. The approach of machine learning is very different. We give you instructions on how to do something instead of giving the computer a set of instructions. For, e.g., think of a program where animal images can be categorized as "cat," "dog," or "mouse." Instead of manually identifying and coding images of these animals for unique features, machine learning incorporates images of these animals and finds features and differences by itself. This machine education process is called instruction.

Deep learning:

Deep learning is a method of machine learning. This utilizes neural networks to understand, so it can sometimes be named deep learning utilizing decision trees, but mostly deep learning requires the use of nerve networks.

Network Neural:

So, what's a network neural? An example here: visualize a neural network as a set of doors one to the next and find yourself to be the' data' to the neural network. Whenever you open a door, you become another person. When you open the last door, you're a very different person. Once you pass the last screen, you become the neural network's "production." In this case, each door represents a layer. So, a neural network is a set of layers that process the input to generate an output in some way.

Sufficient theory, deployment, and configuration This tutorial is for Tensorflow 1.2.1 and Python 3.6. You may also want to look at the official installation guide before following it.

Python

Tensorflow programs are written in Python, which you can download at https://www.python.org/downloads/

You can choose from Python 3 or Python 2, although I highly recommend you install a newer version of 3.5, mainly because these models are already fitted with an optimized PIP kit. Otherwise, you must also mount it.

Tensorflow Installing Python is the next step. Open a command line as an administrator!) (and write:

pip3 install --upgrade tensorflow

If you want to test the installation, write this:

python

>>> import tensorflow as tf

>>> hello = tf.constant('Hello, Tensorflow')

>>> sess = tf.Session()

>>> print(sess.run(hello))

You should see a "Hello, Tensorflow" output now.

Congrats! Welcome! You have just studied Tensorflow's theoretical foundations and set up everything to dig deeper into this problem. Below is for image processing and initiation recognition

IMAGE CLASSIFICATION

The topics in this section are image recognition and classification. Using the start-v3 model, we begin the classification of images with the pre-trained ImageNet data set of Google. Let's continue. Let's start.

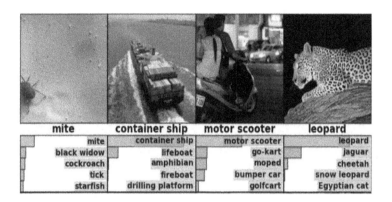

mite	container ship	motor scooter	leopard
mite	container ship	motor scooter	leopard
black widow	lifeboat	go-kart	jaguar
cockroach	amphibian	moped	cheetah
tick	fireboat	bumper car	snow leopard
starfish	drilling platform	golfcart	Egyptian cat

image classification

What is the inception-v3 model?

The Inception v3 model has been pre-trained for the ImageNet Large Visual Recognition Challenge using 2012 data and can distinguish between 1,000 different classes, such as' cat," dishwasher,' "plane."

The TensorFlow team already prepared a tutorial on how to execute the image classification on your machine. Nevertheless, I'll show you as well.

Image classification on the pre-trained ImageNet data set

Well, as we aren't starting from scratch, start by cloning the Tensorflow model's repository from GitHub. Run the following commands:

```
git clone https://github.com/tensorflow/models.git
cd models/tutorials/image/imagenet
python classify_image.py
```

If you haven't installed Git yet, download it here.

classify_image.py downloads the trained model from Google's backend when the program runs the first time. You'll need about 200 MB of free space available on your hard disk.

The above commands classify a panda bear image provided.

If the model is running correctly, the script will generate the following output:

the giant panda, panda, panda bear, coon bear, Ailuropoda melanoleuca (score = 0.88493) indri, indris, Indri indri, Indri brevicaudatus (score = 0.00878)

lesser panda, red panda, panda, bearcat, Ailurus fulgens (score = 0.00317)

custard apple (score = 0.00149)

earthstar (score = 0.00127)

If you want to provide other images, you can do so by editing the argument—image file:

python classify_image.py --iAmAdifferentImage.jpg

That wasn't so tough, wasn't it? But don't worry, it's going to be more difficult. The above template helps us to identify photographs by the Google team into pre-trained groups. But what if you were to retrain our own classes in the beginning?

Last step of Retrain Inception for specific categories

Inception's layer model

Setup

Four additional groups, named "circle," "line," "plus," and "triangle," we would introduce to the Inception layout.

Start by cloning my GitHub folder, type:

git clone https://github.com/koflerm/tensorflow-image-classifier.git

After you have cloned the above repository, we must somehow tell Inception what the right label is for each image.

Since we determine if an entity is a triangle, rectangle, plus, or circle, we need to create a directory called "training dataset" and fill it with four subfolders named after the class mark. These folders will contain data sets (images) for the subjects to be classified for.

```
/
---                                                    /training_dataset
|                                                                      |
|                                        ---                    /circle
|                          |                              circle1.jpg
|                     |                          circle_small_red.png
|                                    |                              ...
|                                                                      |
|                                        ---                    /square
|                                                            square.jpg
|                                                           square3.jpg
|      ...
176
```

Next, we need the data set for the training phase to be used. Because it's really time-consuming to import files manually, we use a "Fatkun Batch Import File" Chrome extension. It enables us to download the first 50 images automatically from the Google image search. Only transfer them to the directories (not appropriate picture format!)

exemplary training images for class "plus."

Executing

After all directories and data sets have been set, let the training begin! Double-click execute the.sh train file. The script installs the model Inception (if not already installed) and retrains the specified image data sets.

```
100 bottleneck files created.
200 bottleneck files created.
300 bottleneck files created.
400 bottleneck files created.
500 bottleneck files created.
600 bottleneck files created.
2017-08-01 09:59:17.258806: Step 0: Train accuracy = 35.0%
2017-08-01 09:59:17.258806: Step 0: Cross entropy = 1.292076
2017-08-01 09:59:17.383817: Step 0: Validation accuracy = 19.0% (N=100)
2017-08-01 09:59:29.591315: Step 100: Train accuracy = 96.0%
2017-08-01 09:59:29.591315: Step 100: Cross entropy = 0.335396
2017-08-01 09:59:29.716326: Step 100: Validation accuracy = 91.0% (N=100)
2017-08-01 09:59:41.861543: Step 200: Train accuracy = 98.0%
2017-08-01 09:59:41.861543: Step 200: Cross entropy = 0.189951
2017-08-01 09:59:41.986558: Step 200: Validation accuracy = 93.0% (N=100)
2017-08-01 09:59:54.096292: Step 300: Train accuracy = 98.0%
2017-08-01 09:59:54.096292: Step 300: Cross entropy = 0.182122
2017-08-01 09:59:54.221307: Step 300: Validation accuracy = 91.0% (N=100)
```

re-training process

177

When the process is completed, about 90 percent of the training accuracy will be returned.

In case you want to take a look, the retrained marks-graphs and the training description will be transferred to the folder called of files.

Now it's time to test the algorithm on our own photos after retraining the software. Download or copy an image into the root directory. Another "triangle" graphic I found. Perform the test by typing:

python classify.py downloadedImage.jpg

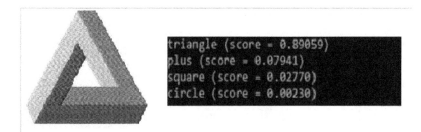

left: downloadedImage.jpg | right: score for each class

Sure, my triangle is graded as a triangle!

(Optional): When you have added certain new class images or subdirectories but do not want to call train.sh and then classify.sh, you can combine the input by typing: (Optional) python retrain.py — bottleneck_dir=tf_files/bottlenecks — how_many_training_steps=500 — model_dir=inception — summaries_dir=tf_files/training_summaries/basic — output_graph=tf_files/retrained_graph.pb — output_labels=tf_files/retrained_labels.txt — image_dir=training_dataset — eval_step_interval=100 & python classify.py image.jpg

Note: image.jpg is the image to be tested

Although the classification works most of the time, there are certain problems:

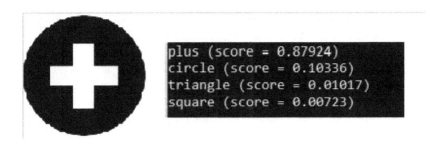

Gets recognized as a plus

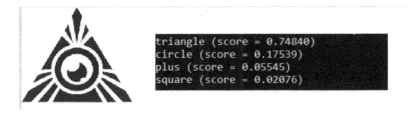

Again, not recognized as a circle

Starting is trained for one-label image classification, so multi-label classification is not possible. If I wanted to classify the above pictures as circles, I just had to use a more precise training set for the class. That's actually a bit longer, the Chrome Extension alone just can't deliver the best results.

All right, we saw that the system did what it should do (most of the time, at least). But how did the cycle of retraining work?

In principle, the script loads the pre-trained Inception v3 model, removes the old top layer, and trains a different one in the geometric forms you want to add. This is called transition teaching — transition learning. The retraining operates in 2 steps— bottleneck and training: in the first step, all disk images are processed, and the bottleneck values for each process are determined. Bottleneck' is an informal term that is used for the layer just before the final classification production sheet. The files are edited to a concise and portable description of the pictures.

The second phase is the actual training of the network's top layer. You can see a number of steps, each demonstrating consistency of preparation, validity accuracy, and entropy cross. The consistency of the training indicates how much of the photos used during the testing is labeled with the correct class. The validation accuracy is the accuracy of a randomly selected set of images. Cross entropy is a loss function that offers an overview of the success of the learning process.

Congratulations, you can now identify pictures using Tensorflow.

INTRODUCTION TO NATURAL LANGUAGE PROCESSING

The essence of natural language processing lies in computers making the natural language understanding. But that's not an easy task. Computers may comprehend the organized types of data, such as spreadsheets and tables in the database, but languages, texts, and voices constitute an unstructured data type and it is challenging for the machine to grasp it, so natural language processing is required.

There are many natural language data in different forms, and it would be very easy for computers to understand and process that data. We can train the models in different ways according to the expected output. Human beings have been writing for thousands of years, there are a number of literary works accessible, and if we let machines realize that it would be fantastic. But the challenge will never be simple. There are numerous difficulties such as recognizing the right meaning of a phrase, proper comprehension of the name of the person, accurate interpretation of the different parts of the voice, resolution of the coreference (in my view the most difficult thing).

Computers can not really understand the language of human beings. If we feed enough data and properly train a model, it can identify and attempt to define various parts of speech on the basis of previously provided data and observations (noun, verb, adjective, supporter, etc.). It tried to make the nearest approximation, which could be embarrassingly wrong a few times when it met a new term.

For a machine, it is very difficult to extract the exact meaning from an expression. For examples, the guy was radiating fire like vibes. The boy had a very inspiring heart, or did he radiate fire? As you can see here, it will be difficult to decode English with a machine.

There are different stages in the preparation of a pattern. To solve a complex problem in machine learning implies to build a pipeline. In simple terms, it means breaking into a number of small problems a complex problem, creating templates for each one, and then combining such models. The specific is being explored in NLP. We should cut the cycle of learning English into several small parts for a layout.

What Is Natural Language Processing? (NLP)

NLP is a way for machines to smartly and usefully interpret, comprehend, and infer significance from human language. By using NLP, developers may arrange and structuralize information for activities such as automated summarization, localization, detection of persons, the abstraction of associations, relational interpretation, speech recognition, and the segmentation of topics.

In How Natural Language Processing Helps Uncover Social Media Sentiment, NLP finds the hierarchical structure of the language to be a clear series of symbols: many words make a phrase, many phrases express concepts and sentences eventually, "says John Rehling. "In evaluating language for its purpose, NLP programs perform valuable long-term tasks, such as grammar corrections and the transcription of language into text, as well as the automated translation of languages." This connection between person and machine facilitates real-world applications such as auto-text summarization, feeling interpretation, subject extraction, recognition of persons, parts of speech labeling, partnership extraction, stemming, and many more. For text mining, machine translation and automated question reply, NLP is commonly used.

NLP is known as a difficult computer science problem. Human language is rarely accurate or spoken clearly. The understanding of human language means not only knowing the words, but also the meanings and how they are related to establishing significance. Despite the fact that language is one of the easiest things the human mind can understand, the complexity of language makes it difficult for machines to master natural language.

What Can Developers Use NLP Algorithms For?

NLP algorithms are used for a variety of applications. They basically allow developers to create a human-language software. Because of the complex nature of human expression, NLP can be hard to learn and execute properly. Nonetheless, you are better equipped to use NLP effectively with the knowledge gained from this post. Some of the project developers may use NLP algorithms to summarize text blocks using Summarizer to extract key ideas while ignoring irrelevant information.

Build a chatbot using Parsey McParseface, a language model that uses Point-of-Speech marks, which parses deep learning.

Automatically generate keyword tags from material by using an AutoTag that utilizes LDA methodology, which identifies topics within a body of the text.

Identify the type of business derived by means of Named Entity Recognition, such as the individual, location, or association.

Using Sentiment Analysis to define the mood of a series, from highly negative to very optimistic.

Reduce terms to their source or core, or split the text into tokens with the use of Tokenizer.

Open Source NLP Libraries

Such libraries provide real-world implementations with the NLP algorithmic building blocks. Algorithmia provides a free API interface to many of these algorithms, with no servers and resources to set up or provide.

Apache OpenNLP: A machine learning toolkit that provides tokenizers, word segmentations, part-speech identifiers, term fragments, chunks, sorting, and more.

Natural Language Toolkit (NLTK): a Library of Python that offers document, sorting, tokenization, hopping, labeling, parsing, and more modules.

Stanford NLP: a range of NLP methods including part-of-speech marking, the object identity called coreference resolution framework, emotion analysis, and more.

MALLET: a Java kit that involves the allocation of latent behavior, content sorting, clustering, subject modeling, knowledge extraction, and more.

A Few NLP Examples

Using Summarizer to replay a block of text immediately, assign subject phrases, and forget everything else.

Generate keyword subject tags from the LDA text, which defines the most relevant words from the document. The Auto-Tag and Auto-Tag URL microservices are based on this method.

Sentiment analysis can be used on the basis of StanfordNLP to define, from very negative to favorable to very optimistic, a thought, perception, or opinion of a sentence. Developers often use an algorithm to classify the emotions of a word or use sentiment analysis to evaluate social media.

NLP algorithms can be very helpful for web developers to provide the key tools necessary to create advanced applications and prototypes.

Example Natural Language Processing Use case

NLP algorithms are typically based on algorithms of machine learning. NLP may rely on machine learning instead of hand-coding large sets of laws to automatically understand such guidelines by analyzing a number of examples (e.g., a large body, like a text, up to a series of phrases) and creating a static conclusion. In addition, the more details, the more specifically the model is evaluated.

Social media research is an excellent example of the use of NLP. Brands monitor online conversations to learn what customers say and gain insight into the actions of people.

"One of the most impressive ways NLP provides precious intelligence is through tracking feelings— tweeting, updating Facebook, etc.— and tagging the text as positive, negative or neutral," Rehling said.

Build Your Own Social Media Monitoring Tool

Get your company name on Twitter using the Retrieve Tweets Using Keyword algorithm. Throughout our situation, we are searching for algorithmic mentions.

Subsequently, pip the data into the Sentiment Analysis method, which assigns 0-4 per string (Tweet).

Facebook also uses NLP to track trends and popular hashtags.

"Hashtags and keywords are two different ways to link and engage in discussions," a software engineer on News Feed, Chris Struhar, said in How Facebook Created Trends for natural language processing. "So don't think Facebook's going to recognize a string as a topic without a hashtag. It's all about NLP: the retrieval of natural languages. A hashtag is not possible, so instead, Facebook searches strings and finds out what strings apply to nodes — network artifacts. We look at the document, and we try to understand. "Not only social media can use NLP for its benefit. Publishers hope that NLP will improve the quality of their online by using technology to "self-filter the offensive comments on the news website to save moderators from what could be a' cumbersome process.'" Francis Tseng, in Prototype winner, said that he used' natural language processing' to solve the problem of journalism's remarks.

Many ease applications of NLP provide remote malicious intrusion tracking, such as phishing, or if someone lies.

Use NLP To Build Your Own RSS Reader

The following algorithms help you to create a machine learning RSS reader in less than 30 minutes: ScrapeRSS to pick up the title and the text of an RSS feed.

Html2Text to preserve the important text, but delete the whole HTML from the paper.

AutoTag utilizes Latent Dirichlet Assignment to classify appropriate document keywords.

Sentiment analyzes are also used to assess whether the essay is optimistic, negative, or neutral.

Finally, Summarizer is used to identify key phrases.

Wrapping up

Natural language processing plays a key role in facilitating human-machine experiences.

As further work in this area is ongoing, we hope to see further breakthroughs that will allow machines intelligent to recognize and understand human language.

DATA CLEANSING

One of the major components of machine learning is data cleaning. This plays an important role in the design of a layout. Computer Cleaning is one of the tasks that everybody does, but nobody thinks about it. It is definitely not the most sophisticated aspect of machine learning, and there are no hidden techniques and mysteries to discover at the same time. Your idea can, however, be easily cleaned or destroyed. Registered data scientists typically spend much of their time here.

"Better data defeats fancier algorithms," thanks to the conviction.

When we have a well-maintained dataset, even with a very simple algorithm, we can obtain desired results, which can sometimes be very useful.

Clearly, numerous types of data require multiple cleaning methods. This systematic approach can, however, always be a good starting point.

Steps involved in Data Cleaning

Removal of unwanted observations

It involves elimination from your sample of duplicate / redundant or meaningless values. Duplicate findings most often arise through data collection, so unrelated results do not really tie into the specific problem you are trying to resolve.

Redundant assumptions significantly change output as the data persists and may attach to the right side or to the wrong side resulting in unfaithful tests.

Every type of data not valuable to us and can be omitted immediately are meaningless findings.

Fixing Structural errors

Structural failures are considered mistakes during the calculation, data transfer, or other similar situations. Structural errors include function typos, same name reference, incorrect groups, i.e., different sections that should really be of the same or contradictory capitalization.

For example, the model treats America and America as different classes or values, although they have the same value or red, yellow, and red-yellow as different classes or attributes. These are certain structural errors that make our model inefficient and yield poor results.

Managing Unwanted outliers

Outliers may trigger certain types of model problems. For starters, linear regression models are less resilient than decision tree models for outliers. We should not generally remove outliers until we have a legitimate reason to remove them. Removing them often improves performance, sometimes not. Therefore you have to have a legitimate reason to remove the outlier, for example, questionable actions that are impossible to be part of real evidence.

Handling missing data

Missing data is a disappointingly difficult problem in machine learning. The missed point can not be dismissed or omitted. They must be carefully handled because they can be an indication of something important. The two most common ways to treat missing data are to replace results from incomplete values.

The deletion of missing values is not optimal because the information is dropped when you drop observations.

The loss of interest can be insightful in itself.

However, in the real world, even if some functionality is absent, you often need to forecast new data!

The missing values from previous observations are imputed.

It is not desirable to impute lost values because the meaning was absent initially, but was filled in, which always contributes to knowledge loss, no matter how advanced the imputation process is.

Once' missing' is almost always descriptive in itself, and if a value is missing, you can say the algorithm.

You don't add real details even if you build a model to impute the principles. You just strengthen the patterns that other features already provide.

Both of these approaches are sub-optimal because if an observation is dropped, data are decreased, and values are imputed, as well as sub-optimal because we record the values, not in the actual dataset which leads to information loss.

Lack of data is like losing a piece of the puzzle. When you lose it, it's like the puzzle space doesn't work. It is like trying to squeeze into an item from another section of the puzzle because you impute it.

The missing data is, therefore, always informative and indicates something important. And by flagging it, we will learn our algorithm of missing data. By using this flagging and filling technique, you essentially allow the algorithm to estimate the optimal missing constant rather than just fill it in with the mean.

Some data cleansing tools:

- ✓ Openrefine
- ✓ Trifacta Wrangler
- ✓ TIBCO Clarity
- ✓ Cloudingo
- ✓ IBM Infosphere Quality Stage

Conclusion

We have therefore, discussed four different data cleaning steps in order to make the data reliable and achieve good results. After the data cleaning measures have been adequately done, we will have a solid dataset that prevents many of the most popular problems. This move should not be hurried because it is of great benefit to the future.

Do not go yet; One last thing to do

If you enjoyed this book or found it useful, I'd be very grateful if you'd post a short review on it. Your support does make a difference, and I read all the reviews personally so I can get your feedback and make this book even better.

Thanks again for your support!

www.ingramcontent.com/pod-product-compliance
Lightning Source LLC
LaVergne TN
LVHW041211050326
832903LV00021B/567